ON THE
SAME
TEAM

Bringing **Educators** & **Underrepresented Families** Together

ARI GERZON-KESSLER

Solution Tree | Press

a division of
Solution Tree

555 North Morton Street
Bloomington, IN 47404
800.733.6786 (toll free) / 812.336.7700
FAX: 812.336.7790

email: info@SolutionTree.com
SolutionTree.com

Visit **go.SolutionTree.com/diversityandequity** to download the free reproducibles in this book.

Printed in the United States of America

Library of Congress Cataloging-in-Publication Data

Names: Gerzon-Kessler, Ari, author.
Title: On the same team : bringing educators and underrepresented families together / Ari Gerzon-Kessler.
Description: Bloomington, IN : Solution Tree Press, [2023] | Includes bibliographical references and index.
Identifiers: LCCN 2023027926 (print) | LCCN 2023027927 (ebook) | ISBN 9781958590010 (paperback) | ISBN 9781958590027 (ebook)
Subjects: LCSH: Early childhood education--Parent participation--United States. | Children of minorities--Education--United States. | Minority families--United States | Home and school--United States. | Community and school--United States. | Child development--United States.
Classification: LCC LB1139.35.P37 G47 2023 (print) | LCC LB1139.35.P37 (ebook) | DDC 372.119/2--dc23/eng/20230913
LC record available at https://lccn.loc.gov/2023027926
LC ebook record available at https://lccn.loc.gov/2023027927

Solution Tree
Jeffrey C. Jones, CEO
Edmund M. Ackerman, President

Solution Tree Press
President and Publisher: Douglas M. Rife
Associate Publishers: Todd Brakke and Kendra Slayton
Editorial Director: Laurel Hecker
Art Director: Rian Anderson
Copy Chief: Jessi Finn
Production Editor: Madonna Evans
Copy Editor: Mark Hain
Text and Cover Designer: Abigail Bowen
Acquisitions Editor: Hilary Goff
Assistant Acquisitions Editor: Elijah Oates
Content Development Specialist: Amy Rubenstein
Associate Editor: Sarah Ludwig
Editorial Assistant: Anne Marie Watkins

ACKNOWLEDGMENTS

This book was made possible thanks to the enduring love, guidance, support, and encouragement of many people I deeply value and appreciate.

To the incredible team at Solution Tree, you consistently exceeded my highest hopes with impressive levels of thoughtfulness, communication, care, and professionalism. Since my first job in a bookstore in 1988 at the ripe age of eleven, it has been a huge dream to have a book published by an esteemed publisher. I am so grateful to Amy Rubenstein, Madonna Evans, Laurel Hecker, and the whole Solution Tree team for their stewardship of the manuscript. They were delightful guides and partners on this journey. A heartfelt thank-you to Douglas Rife for his early enthusiasm for this book and belief in the power and potential of Families and Educators Together (FET) teams as a promising structure for all school communities.

To my one-of-a-kind facilitation mentor and Zen teacher, Diane Musho Hamilton, for regularly modeling how to create the conditions in which high levels of cohesion can be fostered across differences. You consistently teach me how to be a coach that holds the whole while honoring the individual.

To my colleagues and friends at Passageworks Institute, thank you for helping me learn, over twenty years of practice together, how to create connective spaces where adults can authentically bring forth their voices.

To Madeline Case and Kristen Davidson, my profound thanks for initiating the FET concept at pilot schools and providing support in the early stages of this effort to create a structure for connection and transformation. I am also grateful to the great practitioners, researchers, and authors in the field of family partnerships who have taught me so much.

My gratitude to Darcy Hutchins at the Colorado Department of Education, a trusted thought partner over the years. A big thank-you as well to Boulder Valley School District leadership for their continued funding and support of the FET initiative, and specifically my colleagues Bianca Gallegos, Berenice Ramirez, Janice Wheeler, Jennie Done, Diane Brenton, Denys Vigil, Ana Silvia Avendaño, and Sam Messier for being such key allies and advocates of this work.

To the many FET leaders I've been privileged to collaborate with, I am deeply grateful for your dedication to finding better ways to partner with families. I appreciate your humility, your eagerness to learn across differences, and your commitment to a more connective and equitable way of collaborating with families. In these tumultuous times in public education, you are the bridge builders we need to take us toward a new chapter in school-family partnerships.

To the hundreds of families who have participated in FET across our school sites, I have learned so much from your experiences, stories, insights, and advice. Thank you for taking the time out of your busy lives to help our schools become more inclusive and just communities. You have taught me time and again that if we create the right conditions for candid sharing, educators can learn so much from the families at their schools.

To the educators on our FET teams, I am constantly moved by your humility, openness to learning from families, and the sheer devotion required to come to a night meeting on top of your demanding school day. Thank you for the vulnerability, authenticity, and flexibility you bring to our gatherings, and for being the family partnership champions we need.

To the school leaders at our FET sites, I can't imagine better partners in this effort. You are outstanding models for school leaders everywhere for how to listen deeply, surrender control, and ensure that family perspectives transform into actual change.

To all the educators and families who will bring this work to life in their school communities in the years ahead, thank you for your deep determination and big hearts in this important endeavor of making room for everyone on the same team.

To my friend and mentor, Edward Moondance, thank you for nurturing in me a deep love for books and the written word since an early age. My thanks as well to my dear friends William Messer, Shannon McGuire, and Timothy Anspach for your continued encouragement of my writing and the quality of your friendship.

To my parents, who bought a typewriter for an aspiring nine-year-old writer. I am thankful for a lifetime of love and support. I am immensely grateful to my father, Mark Gerzon, who helped me with this book in so many small and significant ways from start to finish. I feel fortunate to be guided by such a seasoned writer and steadily supported by a man who is both a dear friend and my only living parent. Words cannot capture my gratitude for your love and support with this book and so much more.

I am forever indebted to my mother, Rachael Kessler, a pioneer in social-emotional learning. You were a major inspiration for this book and all my other efforts to improve our educational landscape. From my days as a student, teacher, and school leader, you taught me that nurturing relationships one conversation at a time is the best pathway to building stronger school communities. I miss you every day.

Both my parents have devoted their lives to being bridge builders across differences, and I can't think of better models of how to bring people's authentic voices more effectively to public spaces in ways that create lasting change. I am also deeply indebted to my four grandparents, who made many sacrifices in their journey as immigrants to the United States.

To my parents-in-law, Wendy Block and Michael Sigman, for all of their thoughtful feedback and steady care for me as a writer, a husband, and a father. A deep bow as well to Melissa Michaels, my stepmother, for her care and resolute belief in me as both a writer and educational change agent.

To my partner in love and life, Sashi Gerzon-Rose, who supported me in countless practical and emotional ways to realize this big dream of mine. She has also patiently and lovingly held down the fort on the hundreds of nights I spent away from our family so that I could support the growth of our FET teams. I am grateful for the unquantifiable ways that you push me to grow and appreciate my devotion to being of service.

To my daughter, Selah Dove Gerzon-Rose, who made her way into this world as this book was unfolding. She was the best early-morning writing companion I could have dreamed of. As I think about her future, I am aware that tremendous efforts are still required to create the kind of school communities we want for our own children. My deep well of love for you in these earliest days of your life has taught me a lot about how dedicated all families are to seeing their child thrive in school and beyond.

Solution Tree Press would like to thank the following reviewers:

Taylor Bronowicz
Seventh-Grade Teacher
Sparkman Middle School
Toney, Alabama

Courtney Burdick
Apprenticeship Mentor Teacher
Spradling Elementary—Fort Smith
   Public Schools
Fort Smith, Arkansas

Doug Crowley
Assistant Principal
DeForest Area High School
DeForest, Wisconsin

John D. Ewald
Education Consultant
Frederick, Maryland

Justin Fisk
Director of World Languages & ELL
Adlai Stevenson High School
Lincolnshire, Illinois

Nathalie Fournier
French Immersion Teacher
Prairie South School Division
Moose Jaw, Saskatchewan, Canada

Amber Gareri
Instructional Specialist, Innovation
   and Development
Pasadena ISD
Pasadena, Texas

Kelly Hilliard
Math Teacher
McQueen High School
Reno, Nevada

Ben Kitslaar
Principal
West Side Elementary School
Elkhorn, Wisconsin

Laurie Warner
PLC Trainer
Deer Valley Unified School District
Phoenix, Arizona

Allison Zamarripa
Reading & Language Arts Curriculum &
   Instructional Specialist
Pasadena Independent School District
Pasadena, Texas

Visit **go.SolutionTree.com/diversityandequity** to download
the free reproducibles in this book.

TABLE OF CONTENTS

Reproducibles are in italics.

CHAPTER 3
Preparing for the Launch

CHAPTER 4
Making Your First FET Meeting a Success

CHAPTER 5
Being a Great Team Leader

CHAPTER 6
Taking Action and Sustaining the Momentum

ABOUT THE AUTHOR

 **Ari Gerzon-Kessler** leads the family partnerships department for the Boulder Valley School District in Boulder, Colorado. He is also an educational consultant working with schools committed to forging stronger school-family partnerships.

Ari has been an educator since 2000, having served as a principal and bilingual teacher. His educational experiences have allowed him to work in a variety of low- and high-performing schools, and affluent and predominantly low-income schools. Ari is a certified Integral Facilitator and leads trainings at the intersection of family partnerships, social-emotional learning, and cultural responsiveness.

In 2006, Ari was a recipient of the Japan Fulbright Memorial Fund. While he was principal, Ari's school received the Governor's Distinguished Improvement Award in 2013. His leadership efforts to strengthen partnerships with underrepresented families and dismantle unjust practices were featured in *Education Week* in 2015. Ari regularly presents at national and international conferences on Families and Educators Together teams and other innovative family partnership best practices.

Ari is author of *Money Fit: Six Steps to Financial Well-Being* (Amazon, 2019) and coauthor of *Have No Career Fear* (Natavi Guides, 2005). He was a contributing writer to *The Five Dimensions of Engaged Teaching* (Solution Tree, 2013). His writing has been featured in a variety of educational publications, including *Educational Leadership* and *Principal Magazine*.

Ari received a bachelor's degree in African American studies from Wesleyan University and a master's degree in instruction and curriculum from the University of Colorado Boulder.

Introduction

Do the best you can until you know better. Then when you know better, do better.

—Maya Angelou

It was the summer of 2017 and I had just become the director of family partnerships for Boulder Valley School District in Boulder, Colorado. I had spent the first sixteen years of my career primarily serving in low-performing schools or in beleaguered districts. By joining Boulder Valley School District, I was now working in one of the highest-performing, revered, and resource-rich districts in the state. However, I quickly discovered that alongside Denver Public Schools, it possessed the largest achievement and opportunity gaps in the state between White students and students of color (Garcia, 2017).

Boulder is a college town nestled up against the Rocky Mountains, a place designated in 2017 as the happiest city in America (Stone, 2017). Nonetheless, like many districts across the United States, we have been wrestling with the legacy of a decades-long failure to narrow achievement and opportunity gaps. Although the district is predominantly comprised of White families, our students hail from eighty countries and speak eighty-six different languages, and 20 percent of our students are Latino. We have tried to reduce the disparities in achievement and access for at least a generation and struggled to implement solutions that work. As our superintendent Rob Anderson said, "Despite tremendous work by our capable and educated educators, we failed to reduce our achievement and opportunity gaps, which disproportionately impact our students of color and those living in poverty" (R. Anderson, personal communication, July 23, 2020). Of course, I wondered what could be done about it. Why are these gaps so ingrained in our school systems, and what might be key pathways to bridging them?

It took me several years to realize that a major underlying cause was a communication and trust gap between our educators and traditionally underserved families. We guessed what these families needed instead of asking them. We used language and cultural barriers as excuses, preserved a safe distance, and maintained conventional strategies for engaging with them.

I remember learning from parent leaders early on the expression "Nothing about us, without us." We had made decisions for so long in isolation and at best offered one token seat at the table for underrepresented families. If we were going to change our existing practices for families and their children, we needed to invite them to share their experiences and insights. Without them, we could not identify our blind spots, biases, and the barriers that were perpetuating the inequities and disconnection.

It became clear that we needed a more effective approach—one that was relationship centered and brought families and educators together to collaboratively transform our schools and district (Mapp, Henderson, Cuevas, Franco, & Ewert, 2022). Somehow, we had to find a way for all of us to get on the same team.

Our Current Reality

As I write this, three years into the COVID-19 pandemic, our public school system is struggling. At both the school and district level, there are unprecedented levels of divisiveness, overwhelm, and fatigue for both families and educators (Kise & Holm, 2022). Politics and culture wars have increasingly entered the classroom, and with them, a cloud of mistrust has descended on the U.S. school system (Pondiscio, 2022). From curricula to reading materials to a host of other areas of schooling, parents are voicing preferences and challenging educators in unprecedented ways. Overall, research indicates that from the 1970s to the early 2000s, families' and society's faith and trust in schools declined. As one study revealed, in 1975, 65 percent of the surveyed population had a "great deal" or "quite a lot" of confidence in public schools; in 2017, only 36 percent shared such confidence (Schultz, 2019). In the fall of 2022, a Gallup poll found that the percentage of adults satisfied with public schools was 42 percent, a twenty-year low (Mahler, 2023). Families are telling us that they deeply value schools' efforts to connect with them, but they do not feel satisfied with the schools' approaches.

Here are a few sobering facts from surveys of thousands of families and educators. They serve as a wake-up call, particularly for all public schools and districts as they grapple with declining enrollment and a host of new and familiar challenges.

- "At the pandemic's start in 2020, trust in grade school teachers stood at 75 percent. Today, it's 64 percent—a troubling all-time low" (Pondiscio, 2022).
- More than 60 percent of K–12 parents and guardians said there was "room for improvement" in the helpfulness, timeliness, and courteousness of the customer service experience with their school district (Arundel, 2022).
- Sixty-six percent of parents with children under the age of eighteen reported some level of parental burnout (Gawlik & Melynk, 2022).
- The majority of educators do not feel "treated like professionals by the public" (Kurtz, 2022), and a whopping 55 percent are thinking about leaving the profession earlier than they had planned (Walker, 2022).

Educators are suffering from a barrage of challenges. A survey of teachers by Merrimack College paints a stark picture of discontent. Teaching has often been ranked one of the most stressful jobs, and educators' stress has only risen since the COVID-19 pandemic struck at the start of the 2020 decade (Kise & Holm, 2022).

Our students are also grappling with an unparalleled level of mental, social, emotional, and academic challenges and a rise in social isolation (Miller & Pallaro, 2022). Forty-four percent of American high school students report persistent feelings of sadness or hopelessness (Natanson, Stein, & Asbury, 2022). In a survey of hundreds of school counselors in 2022, 94 percent said students demonstrate more signs of anxiety and depression than prior to the pandemic, and 88 percent said students were experiencing more challenges regulating their emotions (Miller & Pallaro, 2022).

In the wake of the pandemic, nondominant students began struggling academically more than their privileged peers (Pondiscio, 2022). As Mapp and colleagues (2022) define the term, "Nondominant families are those affected by systemic oppression, such as being marginalized based on race, class, language, or immigration status" (p. 18). Overall, U.S. fourth-grade test scores contained the worst drop in reading and mathematics scores in decades, a closely watched indicator of our educational and economic trajectory (Chapman & Belkin, 2022). As results from the national assessment of students' reading and mathematics performance revealed, the pandemic exacerbated long-standing disparities and gaps between Black, Latino, Indigenous, and low-income students and their White, middle- and upper-class peers (Chapman & Belkin, 2022). For instance, "By 2022, the typical student in the poorest districts had lost three-quarters of a year in math, more than double the decline of students in the richest districts" (Kane & Reardon, 2023). Even prior to the pandemic, Black, Latino, and low-income students were two to three years of learning behind White students of the same age (National Center for Education Statistics, 2022).

"Perhaps the most effective way to provide an environment that allows for children to flourish, learn and develop is to understand the specific vulnerabilities of immigrant families in the United States. In other words, to care," writes Gabrielle Oliveira (2022), professor of education at Harvard. "Schools aren't only about the hopes of individuals but also the larger hope that we can create an inclusive and just society where people of all sorts of backgrounds can thrive" (Oliveira, 2022, p. SR9).

Approximately twenty million children in the United States have an immigrant parent, comprising 27 percent of the child population. They are the fastest-growing group among U.S. students. As a result, it has become even more crucial that our schools better learn to meet the needs of these students and families (DeParle, 2023).

Schools are not revamping their approaches to engaging with families fast enough to meet the shifting demographics (Meckler & Rabinowitz, 2019). Educators are falling back on antiquated and status quo family involvement approaches that are typically school centric (Santana, Rothstein, & Bain, 2016). This should not come as a surprise, with studies confirming that partnering with families is often the area teachers feel least confident about, in part because of how little training they have in this realm (Hong, 2019; MetLife, 2013).

We clearly stand at a crossroads. This is a moment of truth for education. Do we want to create school communities trapped in the inertia that characterizes many public institutions? Are we unwilling to move beyond the types of school-family approaches that we are familiar with? Or do we have the foresight and determination to make this "moment of disruption . . . a moment of reinvention," as David Brooks (2023) suggests in his article, "America Should Be in the Middle of a Schools Revolution"? Partnering more effectively with families is one of the keys to addressing many of these challenges.

The Importance of Families

During the pandemic, as virtual learning necessitated greater outreach, schools discovered the benefits of forging stronger ties with families. They saw that a phone call home can spark a relationship with families that helps a student re-engage or excel. In a 2021 survey, four out of five educators said their communication with families increased after the pandemic began and that the rise in communication had a positive impact on academic outcomes (Klein, 2021). Author Anya Kamenetz (2022) adds:

> Schools in the United States undeniably learned and grew from the pandemic, in ways that were both humane and innovative. Teachers learned more about what students were going through at home; parents knew more about what teachers were doing and gained more confidence to help. (p. 319)

However, with the resumption of in-person learning, schools have mostly returned to their old ways of engaging with families (Mapp & Bergman, 2021).

Research has shown that strong school-family partnerships positively impact student achievement and well-being, foster greater equity, and act as pillars of great schools (Epstein & Associates, 2018). Nonetheless, this component of school transformation is often relegated to the bottom of the priority list for many schools and districts.

Pedro Noguera, an insightful voice on equity, has watched closely since the 1990s countless reforms fail to achieve their intended outcomes. He shared these sentiments in a speech in 2021:

> Parents are often overlooked, treated as an afterthought. All the research shows that parents matter and have a big role in the lives of their children. All you have to do is look at the students who are doing best in school and you see a lot of parental support. So the issue is: How do we get more parents involved? And how do we build relationships with parents that are rooted in trust and respect? This is an area that needs a lot more attention than it gets right now. Too many schools believe they can do this work in spite of the parents or without them, and it never works. (Noguera, 2021)

Maintaining our traditional practices will not meet the needs of our families or serve our deepest goals as educators. We can't have families peripheral to the real work. We can't continue to "blame each other for any struggles that arise" (Hong, 2019, p. 5). The progress we seek depends on educators and families forging stronger and more authentic partnerships.

For some students and families, a K–12 education has served as the great equalizer and a pathway to the American dream (Benigni, Haeffner, & Lehman, 2022). For others, our schools have perpetuated inequities and long-standing achievement and opportunity gaps (Clark-Louque, Lindsay, Quezada, & Jew, 2019).

The role education can play in creating a more just society is what inspired me to become a teacher and later a principal. In both roles, I experienced firsthand how schools can underestimate the important role that families can play—not just in narrowing gaps but in a host of other crucial pathways to student growth and school transformation. It also became clear that partnerships between underrepresented families and educators are likely to be superficial without a structure for ongoing connection and collaboration.

The efforts unfolding in other countries to create teams that bring families and educators together serve as a model or inspiration. For instance, journalist Karan Deep Singh (2022) has written about the education reforms in Delhi, India, that have been driven by "school management committees, groups of parents, teachers and local officials that provided a platform for airing concerns" and holding the system accountable in monthly meetings (p. A8). Since those committees launched in 2016, students in Delhi have consistently "achieved significantly better scores than their peers countrywide in English, science, mathematics and social sciences" (Singh, 2022, p. A8). We need to move beyond random acts of parent involvement to a more systematic process, which means "moving from where we are now—a scattered, marginal, and unaligned set of programs and policies—to more strategic and systemic approaches to family and community engagement" (as cited in Clark-Louque et al., 2019, p. 23).

Family Involvement Versus Authentic Partnerships

Schools typically engage with families in conventional ways when it comes to forging relationships. They offer the same events every year to preserve these comfortable arrangements. For many decades, the dynamic between schools and families has been driven by an involvement approach rather than one based on mutual partnership. The family involvement approach is often characterized by a focus on one-way communication, with staff telling parents what they think families need to know, or what some refer to as "leading with the mouth" (Ferlazzo, 2011, p. 12). This stance is often characterized by telling families how they can contribute and sharing with them the needs and goals that the staff have defined in isolation. The focus in the involvement model is not on listening to families. The focus tends to be on activities or events rather than relationship building or creating true cultural change within schools (Hong, 2019). *Family involvement* was the conventional term before it shifted to *family engagement.*

Engagement is a step in the right direction, but it still reflects a top-down approach and a focus on such things as attendance at parent-teacher conferences or how well families support the academic and behavior expectations placed on students (Pondiscio, 2022). While *family engagement* is still used by some experts and practitioners, even the phrase itself places too much weight on families when the greater onus needs to be on educators (Tschannen-Moran, 2014). Consequently, instead of *engagement*, throughout this book I will be using the term *partnerships*. It speaks better to the mutuality and deeper alliance needed to propel our schools forward.

Authentic school-family partnerships prioritize listening to families, honoring them as experts, and collaborating with them as equal partners (Weiss, Lopez, & Caspe, 2018). Susan Auerbach (2012), one of the leading experts on authentic partnerships, defines them as "respectful alliances among educators, families, and community groups that value relationship building, dialogue across difference, and sharing power in pursuit of a common purpose in socially just, democratic schools" (p. 29).

Table I.1 is a synthesis of the school-family partnerships approach that we need to implement in our schools. As you will see, the vision around authentic partnerships stands in stark contrast to what conventional family involvement looks, feels, and sounds like. Please also see appendix B (page 127) for a reproducible "Moving Toward Authentic Family Partnership" rubric.

Engaging families is one of the keys to transforming schools and districts from good to great (Bryk, Sebring, Allensworth, Luppescu, & Easton, 2010). Since the early days of the COVID-19 pandemic, educators have realized that strengthening partnerships is an essential component to effective teaching, student growth, and school improvement (Constantino, 2021). So why is it then that more schools and districts are not systematically implementing school-family partnership best practices?

The Barriers to Partnerships

In some ways, schools are designed to fail in their efforts to partner effectively with underrepresented families (Winthrop, 2022). As change expert Michael Fullan (2007), one of our greatest voices on school improvement, puts it, "Nowhere is the two-way street of learning more in disrepair and in need of social reconstruction than in the relationship among parents, communities and their schools" (p. 190).

Schools are social and cultural institutions, and as such, they fail to build strong ties with nondominant families because they "oftentimes reflect, reinforce, and reify the illness and inequity of the larger society" (Hong, 2019, p. 157). Put more simply, schools were designed to perpetuate White, middle-class values and ways of being (Nomensen, 2018). This, in turn, has caused the long-standing and often unaddressed history of

Table I.1: Family Involvement Versus Authentic Partnerships

Family Involvement	Authentic Partnerships
One-way, transactional relationships	Two-way, authentic relationships
Do "to" families	Do "with" families
Goals and activities focused	Relationships focused
Surface-level trust	High-level trust
Random acts of outreach and connection	Relationship-building systems embedded in the school culture
One-time projects	Sustained and well-integrated projects
Hierarchical leadership	Shared leadership
Maintaining the status quo	Oriented toward transformation
Avoiding issues of power	Examining and changing power dynamics
Student learning is teacher's responsibility	Student learning is shared responsibility
Family cultures are overlooked or devalued	Family cultures are considered, included, and valued
Communication using traditional forms, such as email, primarily in English	Communication using multiple forms, in several languages
Meetings focused on what parents should do	Meetings focused on how school and families can work together

Source: Clark-Louque et al., 2019; Ferlazzo, 2011; Ishimaru, 2020; Zeichner, Bowman, Guillen, & Napolitan, 2016.
*Visit **go.SolutionTree.com/diversityandequity** for a free reproducible version of this table.*

distrust and antagonism between schools and families of color (Dugan, 2022). As Karen Mapp and colleagues (2022) conclude in *Everyone Wins*:

> Schools have historically been marginalizing institutions—places where parents can be haunted by their own traumatic experiences—that leave parents out of decision-making or actively push parents away, that prioritize professional expertise, and do not reflect the diversity of the communities they serve. (p. 88)

Despite our best intentions, many schools and educators continue to blame families who do not comply with their vision of what involvement should look like. Additionally, reforms that are aimed at creating "better schools," especially for low-income students and students of color, continue to fail because educators avoid addressing one of the larger barriers to progress—deeply rooted "relational, structural, and contextual distrust" between schools and the communities they serve "that impedes educational change"

(Schultz, 2019, p. 141). Consequently, the absence of strong school-family partnerships exacerbates inequities (Santana et al., 2016). Noguera (2018) uses the compelling analogy of a garden to capture how our approach is askew:

> In a garden, if you get the conditions right, everything grows. If the vegetables don't grow, you don't blame the vegetables. How often do you see students and parents being blamed for low achievement versus us [educators] asking ourselves: Did we create the right conditions?

In too many schools and districts, we are not creating the right conditions due to lack of will or skill, and because of ingrained beliefs that limit possibilities for all stakeholders. While promising examples of partnerships abound, and the shared purpose of supporting a child's development provides an obvious tie between families and educators, we do ourselves a disservice if we pretend that parents and teachers are on the same page from day one. "More often than not, parents and teachers feel estranged from and suspicious of each other," writes Sara Lawrence-Lightfoot, professor of education at Harvard. "Their relationship tends to be competitive and adversarial rather than collaborative and empathic. Their encounters feel embattled rather than peaceful and productive" (as cited in Sanders & Sheldon, 2016, p. 36).

While Lawrence-Lightfoot's assessment paints a skeptical picture, it offers a helpful reminder that building strong ties requires thoughtfulness and significant effort. The garden is not fertile ground from the opening moments of back-to-school night; we must steadily cultivate it with great intentionality every day of the school year. Since schools are hierarchical and educators possess more positional power than families, they hold the lion's share of the responsibility in building and sustaining a partnership that overcomes these inherent challenges (Tschannen-Moran, 2014).

By becoming more conscious of the obstacles to stronger partnerships and how they manifest in our day-to-day actions within schools, we automatically unlock insights into some of the next steps or solutions. Before we look at the barriers for families, let's look at the barriers for educators, which are far more entrenched.

Barriers for Educators

Educators say that engaging with families is the most challenging of their responsibilities (Mapp, Carver, & Lander, 2017). For instance, in a 2022 survey, 52 percent of teachers stated that it was not easy to communicate about difficult academic or behavioral issues. Forty-three percent said it was difficult to "establish strong relationships with families" (Mapp & Bergman, 2021, p. 2). There are numerous reasons why educators are not set up for success in partnering with families. To create a foundation for stronger collaboration, it is crucial for us to examine some of the major obstacles that limit educators in their part of this often lopsided dynamic.

Lack of Confidence, Training, and Time

One of the barriers educators face regarding family engagement is a lack of confidence. When asked by researchers what facet of their role they most lacked confidence in, both teachers and principals identified family engagement (MetLife, 2013).

Another major reason that educators often feel intimidated, insecure, or unprepared is because they have typically received minimal training on how to effectively partner with families (Hong, 2019). In fact, less than one in five teachers received training on family engagement in their pre-service programs (Bergman, 2022). Fewer than one-third of states require learning about effective family engagement strategies in order to become a teacher (National Association for Family, School, and Community Engagement, 2020b). As a result, educators are often unaware of the potential fruits of investing more time and energy in partnering with families. Additionally, teachers, school leaders, and other school staff rarely receive informal guidance or evaluative feedback on how they are progressing in their collaboration with families (Hong, 2019).

Most educators have not witnessed excellent family partnerships in schools and have not been trained or expected to improve their practice over time. Therefore, they don't necessarily have a clear picture of what this work looks like or how it can make their jobs easier. To build a new mental model, educators need support through a scaffolded learning journey (Bergman, 2022).

The sheer overwhelming nature of the work, regardless of one's role in a school, translates into limited time each day to build relationships or communicate with families. Educators also typically do not work for school leaders who devote time or allocate other resources for them to engage in effective partnership practices, such as home visits or positive phone calls (Auerbach, 2012). While teachers hold the greatest responsibility for partnering with families because they know their students and families best, it is their principal's responsibility to provide the time, support, training, and expectations (Bergman, 2022).

Even though research shows that interactive experiences with families often build educators' capacity more effectively than trainings (Mapp & Bergman, 2021), most school staff who want to implement best practices must do so on their own time, turning these highly effective relationship-building efforts into add-ons to their already hectic jobs (Dugan, 2022). As Hong (2019) writes, most teachers and school administrators "argue that 'there's no extra time in the day for this,' 'my teachers are already doing so much,' or 'we can work on this later, but we have some other priorities now'" (p. 181).

Limiting Beliefs and Perspectives

Educators' belief systems and perspectives about families are another fundamental barrier to transforming the status quo and moving toward more authentic family partnerships (Ishimaru, 2020). Here are six ways that we as educators can get in our own way and limit the possibilities for meaningful connections with families.

1. **Maintaining biased perspectives:** Maintaining deficit views or biases leads to a plethora of assumptions and limits our capacity to effectively partner with families (Clark-Louque et al., 2019). For instance, in a 2022 survey, 73 percent of teachers believed "some families are just not interested in supporting their child's education" (Bergman, 2022, p. 8). A biased perspective is often conjoined with a perception of apathy on the part of families or a limiting, one-dimensional belief that caring is everything when it comes to fostering strong engagement. This often sounds like, "If families cared more," then everything would magically improve.

2. **Operating from a place of anxiety:** Some educators may have an anxiety or fear of "messing up" because they did not grow up in the communities that they serve and may possess limited knowledge, experience, and understanding of the cultures and historical context of the students and families (Bergman, 2022). This can be additionally problematic when combined with biases, judgments, or unproductive expectations that nondominant families conform to the behaviors of White, middle-class parents (Ishimaru, Bang, & Valladares, 2019). Relatedly, some educators believe that certain families hold deficit views of them as educators and blame them for their child's struggles at school (Schaedel et al., 2015).

3. **Failing to establish trust:** Failure to begin relationships with families from the firm ground of trust inhibits school-family partnerships. One study on trust in family-school relationships found that parents tend to have higher trust levels in educators than educators hold for parents (Tschannen-Moran, 2014).

4. **Undervaluing school-family partnerships:** Lacking awareness of the value of school-family partnerships and its links to learning impedes positive outcomes for students (see figure 6.2, page 94). This can lead educators to fall back on their own decades-old memories of how their teachers engaged with their families to inform their approach to students' families. This mental model is defined by a preference that families offer support from afar and only when asked (Mapp et al., 2017).

5. **Taking too much responsibility:** Holding onto the misguided belief in the "tangible triad"—the notion that fostering strong engagement practices hinges solely on teachers, students, and parents—fails to acknowledge the vital role that school administrators, support staff, extended family, and community members often play in forging strong partnerships (D. Hutchins, personal communication, February 25, 2021).

6. **Being unwilling to take chances:** Educators should be willing to surrender to the vulnerability, uncertainty, and risk in giving families more influence or meeting families in a spirit of greater mutuality, even if it means disrupting the status quo of schools (Ishimaru, 2020).

Lack of District Support

The ways that most districts and schools operate also impedes their ability to move steadily toward more authentic partnerships. Several factors are often in play at a district level that impede the growth of partnership practices:

- Failing to allocate funds, time, or other resources to help move schools beyond standard practices, such as not having designated people to coordinate efforts at a district level, or not having family liaisons at the school level (Constantino, 2021)

- Neglecting to train or expose upper leadership to the benefits of strong school-family partnerships

- Maintaining the status quo and thus preserving significant barriers to systemic change (Budge & Parrett, 2022)

- Having a defensive or reactive stance in which the bulk of upper leadership's focus on families is centered on the most vocal parents or the "squeaky wheels"

- Failing to develop policies and district-level plans for improving partnerships or assessing ongoing efforts

- Overwhelming school-based staff with many initiatives that limit their time to focus on strengthening relationships with families

- Operating in silos at a district level, which often translates to school-family partnership efforts happening in isolation rather than being integrated into existing district initiatives

Another reason why more schools and districts are not on the pathway to exemplary practices is their inability to communicate about school-family partnerships with all stakeholders, particularly decision makers such as principals and district leaders. Regardless of our role in the education system, including those of us who specialize in the work, we lack a common and compelling definition of authentic school-family partnerships (Constantino, 2021). We are rarely able to skillfully articulate how true partnerships differ from traditional understandings of family involvement, and do not communicate its importance effectively.

Barriers for Families

Underrepresented families are often hesitant to engage with schools because of a host of existing barriers. Since many U.S. educators do not come from underrepresented backgrounds, it can be hard for them to anticipate the needs or have awareness of the challenges that some families experience in our schools.

Cultural Differences

Here are seven key barriers that schools need to consider as they chart a path toward better partnerships with families.

1. The school staff's lack of familiarity with families' languages and cultural backgrounds (Cadogan, 2022)

2. Constraints on families' time (second and third jobs) or mobility (living far from the school or relying on public transportation) (Cadogan, 2022)

3. Lack of citizenship status (Santana et al., 2016)

4. Maintaining a distance from teachers and school staff out of deference and different cultural expectations of parent-teacher roles (for example, viewing educators as authority figures who are not to be questioned)

5. Low levels of trust for school staff because of their own experiences as either students or caretakers

6. Feelings of being disrespected, dismissed, unseen, and devalued (Cashman, Sabates, & Alcott, 2021) and that teachers blame them when their child has difficulties at school (Constantino, 2021)

7. The perception that they are difficult, confrontational, or inappropriate when they question or challenge existing school practices (Ishimaru, 2020)

Overall, underrepresented families are eager to build or deepen their partnerships with schools. For instance, one study that looked specifically at Latino families concluded, "Far from being disengaged, Latino parents, more than any other demographic, strongly agree (58%) that family engagement from schools is essential to their student's success" (Learning Heroes, 2021).

However, schools are not doing enough to meet these needs. A 2021 survey revealed that nearly half of Latino parents (48 percent) said they do not have people they can talk to in their community about their child's learning. The same percentage said they do not know how to start conversations with educators about learning challenges their child has experienced (UnidosUS, 2022).

Unwelcoming School Environments

Schools tend to plan everything unilaterally, even events for families. When I take an unvarnished look back at my six years as a school principal, I feel both embarrassment and regret that we rarely brought families to the decision-making table. We did not even include their expert voices when we planned events such as back-to-school nights or parent-teacher conferences. By failing to include family perspectives, we consistently missed out on the opportunity to improve these events for all stakeholders.

Our approach, similar to the majority of schools and districts, was based on an assumption that schools know what is best for children and families (Hong, 2019). However, the reality is that "reshaping systems toward educational justice means that key decisions that impact students and families need to be made with them, not for them" (Ishimaru, 2020, p. 93).

Schools often remain bureaucratic and transactional institutions that intentionally or unintentionally keep families at a distance. Many underrepresented families have commonly had the experience of feeling alienated by the bureaucratization of schooling and lack of familiarity with the politics and processes of schools (Oliveira, 2022; Santana et al., 2016). Additionally, many families have simply not been exposed to strong examples of school-family partnerships at any school that they or their child has attended.

As we see across various sectors of society, and not just in schools, it is often harder for an institution to change than the people who use the institution. This close look at the current reality and existing barriers helps us understand why so many American schools have by default remained in the family involvement stance rather than pursuing the authentic partnerships approach that leads the entire school community to thrive.

Rather than focusing disproportionately on the barriers to partnerships, we should spend more time transforming the outdated practices that schools have perpetuated. As Mapp and colleagues (2022) found in a detailed review of fifteen studies:

> Real possibilities for partnerships emerge when [educators] move from just *thinking* differently about engagement to permanently *transforming* their practice. In particular, both teachers and school leaders are able to shift how they communicate with families and integrate families' wisdom and knowledge into their practice. (p. 51)

The Benefits of Partnerships

Decades of research, as well as experience in the field, confirm that the schools that thrive, including high-poverty schools, are places where authentic school-family-community partnerships are integrated into the culture of the school (Sanders & Sheldon, 2016). This often occurs because leaders of these schools embrace partnerships as a systemic strategy, have a comprehensive plan that incorporates that strategy into the school infrastructure, and make it an essential condition for teaching and learning (Mapp et al., 2022).

In their in-depth study of Chicago schools, Anthony Bryk and colleagues (2010) discovered that strong ties between schools and families were one of the five key levers for improving schools from good to great. When strong school-family partnerships or any of the other four elements were removed, the school would not improve. Cultivating strong relationships and engaging in frequent communication between school staff and families are arguably the most effective pathways to improving school culture. In addition, prioritizing relationships is a more culturally responsive approach because some underrepresented families may identify with collectivist value systems, which emphasize relationships over tasks (El Yaafouri, 2022). Table I.2 (page 14) summarizes some of the most significant benefits for all partners.

Table I.2: Benefits of Positive Collaborative Relationships

Benefits for Students	Benefits for Families	Benefits for Schools
Improved health, social and emotional well-being, and social and cognitive skills (Mapp et al., 2022)	Development of leadership abilities and feeling more included and connected to the school (Mapp et al., 2022)	Educators find more joy in their work and demonstrate improved attitudes and morale (Constantino, 2021)
Lower rates of student anxiety, aggression, and depression (Mapp et al., 2022)	Access to institutional knowledge and resources, which improves ability to support their child's academic success (Santana et al., 2016)	Educators are more likely to stay at schools where they have strong partnerships with families (Mapp et al., 2017) and remain in the profession longer (Mapp et al., 2022)
Better grades, attendance rates, test scores, and increased likelihood that students go to college or a postsecondary program (Jargon, 2022)	Provision of a community hub and peer network	Educators and staff improve relationships with families and community (Mapp & Bergman, 2021)
Reduced dropout rates and increased graduation rates (Ishimaru, 2020; Mapp, 2021)	More likelihood that school-related needs and concerns are addressed (Mapp et al., 2022)	Educators gain insights into students' strengths and can be more effective at motivating and engaging students (Mapp et al., 2022)
Improved behavior and fewer discipline issues (Epstein & Associates, 2018)	Higher levels of trust (Pondiscio, 2022)	Educators feel less isolated and a sense of shared purpose
Faster rates of literacy acquisition and growth in mathematics (Mapp et al., 2022)	A greater sense of agency	Schools perform better, have a more positive culture, and develop better reputations (Mapp et al., 2022)
Greater sense of safety and security (Oliveira, 2022)	Access to strategies to support their child's learning at home	Educators and staff develop more multicultural and community awareness and value families more (Mapp et al., 2022)
More successful transitions from one phase of education to the next (Epstein & Associates, 2018)	Stronger and more trusting relationships with educators at their school	Community partners become more involved in supporting the aspirations of students, staff, and families

At the heart of strengthening school-family partnerships is bridging the growing divides between affluence and poverty, between White people and people of color, between English speakers and English learners, and between family and school. When there is trust and collaboration between educators and families, children feel it. They feel accepted and valued. They feel known. Then school and home are like parentheses, with children nested inside a community that feels connected rather than fragmented. In that kind of quality environment, learning feels safer.

With great intentionality and determination, educators and families need to challenge current paradigms of family engagement and co-create this shift toward authentic partnerships (Budge & Parrett, 2022). By doing so, schools will more effectively address the array of challenges and better meet their potential. As educational activist Parker Palmer (1998) writes, "People who start movements do so not because they hate an institution but because they love it too much to let it descend to its lowest form" (p. 170).

We need to equip educators with efficient, high-leverage practices that help them build stronger relationships with families, enhance learning outcomes, and transform school communities. This book showcases Families and Educators Together (FET) teams, a structure that supports the effective implementation of strong school-family partnership practices, and shows you how to implement FET teams in your school or district. FET is centered on the creation and efforts of teams, comprised of family members, educators, and school leaders, that meet regularly to engage in candid dialogue and team-building activities that forge trust, spark mutual learning, and ultimately lead to collaborative action.

After decades of insufficient progress, schools need to prioritize better serving underrepresented students and families, particularly from Latino, Black, and Indigenous backgrounds. Structures like FET are increasingly needed as more immigrant families and families of color attend U.S. schools. For instance, one in four children in the United States was born in another country or has at least one parent who was (Oliveira, 2022). In 2022, Latino students comprised 28 percent of the U.S. school-age population (compared to just 9 percent in the 1980s), and they will make up one-third of our student population by 2030 (UnidosUS, 2022). More robust support for underrepresented families "will enhance all learning communities and create more accessible opportunities for engagement" (UnidosUS, 2022).

Having coached dozens of team leaders and codesigned and cofacilitated more than four hundred FET gatherings, I have witnessed firsthand the impact that forming these vital partnerships has on students, families, educators, and school communities.

FET incorporates a multitude of elements that are essential to both thriving family-school-community partnerships and underrepresented families benefiting in a host of ways. Some of the core components of strong partnership efforts include the commitment of district leadership, examining inequities head-on, putting parent voices at the center of ongoing change efforts that are grounded in a shared leadership approach, and regular reflection on progress and areas for improvement (Sheldon, 2021).

Additionally, since FET is centered on underserved families who have often been on the margins of our schools, it is shaped by the three culturally sustaining approaches that partnerships expert Soo Hong (2019) articulates in her book *Natural Allies: Hope and Possibility in Teacher-Family Partnerships*. These approaches are as follows.

- Repair relationships through the development of relational trust and healing.
- Renew perspectives by bringing new voices into the conversation.
- Reinvent the school with a vision for family and community engagement (Hong, 2019).

FET is further informed by the five research-based aims of the Family Leadership Design Collaborative that Ann Ishimaru and colleagues (2019) propose. These five research-based aims are as follows.

- Start with families' and communities' priorities, not the school's agenda.
- Recognize and treat families of color as experts on their own children.
- Give families and communities the resources, time, and space to envision solutions, not just share their pain.
- Help families and educators learn to facilitate meetings across racial, cultural, and other differences.
- Ensure families have real influence on important educational decisions (Ishimaru et al., 2019).

What's in This Book

On the Same Team provides a unique and innovative template for educator collaboration with underrepresented families. In the following chapters, we will explore what FET is, the outcomes it produces, the research that informs it, and the keys to planning engaging and effective FET meetings. This book will show you how to strengthen ties between your school and families and create a more welcoming and connected school for all.

Chapter 1 presents a deep dive into the concept of FET teams. We will explore the goals and activities of FET teams, how they are distinct from other school teams, and their potential impacts for all stakeholders. We will also look at the four pillars of building authentic school-family relationships.

Chapter 2 considers the team itself: who is on it and why, how to put the team together, and the importance of having a devoted district lead and team leaders. It explores how to garner strong buy-in as you recruit team members and explains the critical role that school leaders play in a successful launch. It also examines the qualities and skills to identify and cultivate in team leaders.

Chapter 3 focuses on the key steps to prepare for the launch of your team. It outlines how to effectively lay the groundwork in the opening weeks of the school year for a strong start. It emphasizes the importance of strong preparation and planning and provides guidelines for executing these vital steps. This chapter also provides advice for training and engaging team leaders and members.

Chapter 4 explores the elements of inspiring and effective FET meetings. This chapter will help you create compelling meeting agendas, feel confident facilitating and organizing a FET meeting, and learn a variety of ways to engage team members.

Chapter 5 explores what outstanding team leaders do and delineates ten habits of effective facilitators. You will learn concrete ways team leaders can prioritize relationship building and serve as effective connectors among team members. You will also learn how leaders can leverage skills such as deep listening and asking skillful questions to garner trust and accelerate the team's progress.

Chapter 6 is centered on what excellent teams do to sustain momentum, from building strong bridges and amplifying parent voices, to embarking on action projects and creating synergy with other school-improvement efforts. It also includes some helpful case studies and key leadership strategies for navigating obstacles and helping FET teams thrive.

This is a handbook for creating more welcoming, cohesive, equitable, and just schools and districts. Each chapter contains practical tools and examples to help you with this work and concludes with a list of reflection questions. The book also includes appendices with numerous resources, such as a frequently asked questions (FAQ) section (page 121), and tools, such as a sample districtwide FET calendar (page 127) and a year-at-a-glance timeline (page 135), to help you along your FET journey. Helpful example stories of FET in action are included in each chapter. Note that personal and school names in some of these stories have been changed for privacy.

Who This Book Is For

This book is primarily for district and school leaders, as they are most likely to initiate the FET process. However, the best practices that inform FET teams are relevant for *all* educators, regardless of their position, experience level, or the demographics of their school or district. Teaching teams and departments can use it as a resource for their continued professional learning and an inspiration for trying new approaches. School leaders can use this book to chart a vision for enhancing school-family partnerships or as a professional development tool in the spring to set the tone for the next school year.

The book is also for parent leaders who want to share a path forward with the staff in their child's school or district. It's worth noting that several FET teams have been launched because a staff member or parent heard about the rewards of making this commitment and brought the concept to their administrator.

District leaders can use this book to propel schools to move from family involvement approaches to more effective school-family partnership efforts. They can use it to guide conversations with other district-level colleagues as well as school and parent leaders about how to steadily strengthen their schools.

If you are concerned that investing time to strengthen family partnerships will feel cumbersome or pointless, my experience has been that the approaches discussed in this book are efficient and deeply impactful. When a small amount of time or money is allocated to these efforts and the will and skill are present, the practices described here are easily replicable and actionable.

The remainder of this book offers a field-proven structure—Families and Educators Together teams—as well as insights and practical strategies for how to achieve the outcomes and overcome the barriers enumerated in this introduction. When we implement these best practices, we can create true transformation that benefits the entire school community. The obstacles to creating positive change are not insignificant, but the benefits of building and deepening partnerships make this pursuit both necessary and profoundly fruitful.

CHAPTER 1

Understanding Families and Educators Together Teams

FET is different. In other schools there was nothing in place to connect us with parents. Here we are family. It's not us and them; it is us together.

—Louisville Middle School Teacher

Now that we have explored the wide range of benefits that partnerships provide students, families, educators, and school communities as a whole, let's take a deeper look at how these outcomes can be achieved. Let's explore what FET is and how it works.

What Is FET?

The ultimate goal of FET is to both transform the school community and cultivate a space where everyone enhances their capacity for relationship building and deepens their commitment to effective partnership practices. When schools commit to a FET team, they quickly move from a scattered approach to one of greater intentionality. They shift from the type of school where a few parents hold power to a more democratic and generative model.

FET integrates and strengthens five areas of education that are often treated separately: (1) school-family-community partnerships, (2) equity and cultural responsiveness, (3) supporting immigrant families and multilingual learners, (4) social-emotional learning (SEL), and (5) improving school culture. Unlike organizations such as the Parent-Teacher Association (PTA) that focus on volunteering, events, and fundraising, FET co-creates changes that lead to more voices being heard by enhancing relationships between educators and underrepresented families.

At schools that do not have a FET team, it is often the school leaders, the teaching staff, or the most vocal and privileged parents driving the change, which often heightens the marginalization of underrepresented families. Conversely, at schools with FET teams, parents who were previously sidelined spearhead change and work side by side with educators.

FET teams provide a consistent forum for collaborating with underrepresented families, which equips them with a deeper knowledge of the inner workings of schools and helps school staff uncover the actual root causes of opportunity gaps. FET is based loosely on the Action Team for Partnerships model out of Johns Hopkins University (Epstein & Associates, 2018). FET teams have catalyzed a notable shift from making assumptions about families' needs to deeply listening, and from guessing what families need to taking shared actions that create a school where everyone feels a strong sense of belonging. At its core, FET builds both educators' and families' capacity for partnerships and cultivates an environment in which meaningful conversations lead to mutual learning. As family partnerships expert Jamila Dugan (2022) writes:

> When families and educators do come together and brainstorm answers around a central question in a way that nurtures dialogue and shared ownership, the solutions are always richer. And when we create those opportunities with families who have been othered or minoritized in mind, we have more opportunities to increase inclusivity. (p. 26)

Historically in America's education system, forums for underrepresented families to bring forth their voices have been limited, have been nonexistent, or, as Auerbach (2012) puts it, have "done little to enfranchise marginalized groups and have instead solidified entrenched power" (p. 33). In addition, dialogue has been an underutilized pathway for helping stakeholders discover new insights, strengthen schools, and narrow gaps between educators and families (Santana et al., 2016).

This failure to create spaces and structures for purposeful collaboration has meant many missed opportunities for innovation or strengthening trust with traditionally marginalized families. Educational visionaries like Paulo Freire (2018) taught us in the 1970s about the transformative power of dialogue, which must be grounded in faith in people and deep hope that change is possible (Knight, 2022). At the start of this century, Peter Senge (2000) called dialogue "the most effective practice we know for team learning" (p. 75), and Linda Darling-Hammond made clear that "the new model of school reform must seek to develop communities of learning grounded in communities of democratic discourse" (as cited in Gibbs, 2006, p. 33).

An important aim of FET is to challenge the status quo. For instance, when a FET team in my Boulder, Colorado, district was considering revamping parent-teacher conferences, the principal said, "We just do it the same way year after year without thinking about it. It's terrible." This kind of humility and candor is only possible in an atmosphere of psychological safety and mutual respect, such as that fostered by FET. Chapter 2 (page 31) will take a closer look at how to put together a FET team, but for now let's look at who comprises a FET team and their overall goals.

Who Is on a FET Team?

A FET team consists of family members from underrepresented communities within the school (most commonly parents but sometimes caretakers or siblings), teachers, the school principal, and sometimes the assistant principal or dean. Other school staff, such as counselors, community liaisons, and campus security, may participate as well. The aim is to have at least five educators (including the principal) and five members from underrepresented families present at each monthly meeting. In our district, participating families are overwhelmingly Latino, but some teams consist of parents from half a dozen different national, cultural, and linguistic backgrounds. While we know that families even within the same cultural or racial group can have vastly different experiences from one another in navigating our schools, underrepresented families from a host of different backgrounds often experience similar challenges. As one Asian parent remarked at a FET meeting attended predominantly by Latino parents, "We have the same types of problems and challenges at school; we just come from different cultures."

What Do FET Teams Do?

FET teams meet one evening a month for ninety minutes. They gather in the evening because this is typically the best time for families. Meetings are usually held in the school library or other communal space, or outside when weather permits it. Schools typically hold meetings in the language of the underrepresented families they're trying to reach, with English interpretation available, but some teams meet in English and have interpretation available in multiple languages. The meeting is facilitated by between two and five FET team leaders, who are usually a combination of staff and parent leaders. The principal is always expected to attend or occasionally will send the assistant principal in their place. Childcare is provided, and a meal is shared.

In addition to engaging in team-building activities, team members share valuable information and discuss questions that shed light on underrepresented families' experiences and spark insights around more effective partnership practices. The topics discussed in FET meetings are later shared with the broader community of families and staff.

Over the course of hundreds of FET gatherings at more than twenty-five different schools, I have learned much about the optimal conditions and structures that help teams thrive. For instance, I have learned that morning meetings are not effective and that one hour is insufficient to achieve intended outcomes. While you may adapt or refine some of these guidelines to make them work for your school or district, they are the result of a continuous process of refinement and reflection on what has worked best for a broad range of teams.

Team meetings center parent voices in ways that benefit the entire school community and lead to mutually beneficial change efforts. By the third or fourth FET meeting of the school year, teams identify one or two action projects that will strengthen the quality of school-family partnerships at their school. These projects might look like refining an existing structure, such as back-to-school night, or creating a new structure for enhancing communication between staff and families, such as a positive phone call system. Teams typically spend one-third to half of the meeting discussing these action projects and bringing them to fruition.

Here are a few examples of the types of action projects that previous FET teams have engaged in.

- An elementary school revamps their parent-teacher conferences to allow families that receive interpretation an equitable amount of time to meet with their child's teacher, and staff are trained on how to host more relationship-centered and reciprocal conferences.

- A middle school assembles a panel of Latino parents that supports staff in learning about their experiences (positive and negative) at the school. The panel offers a host of insights that drive the staff's professional development session on strengthening partnerships with underrepresented families.

- A high school creates a Facebook page in Spanish that helps Latino families become more informed about key information from the school and communicate more easily with school staff.

- A middle school learns that families want more communication from staff in their preferred language and pathways to communicate more easily with the staff. This leads to the staff-wide implementation of an app that enables texting across linguistic differences.

- A high school realizes that for many years Latino families have not felt equipped with key information to support their child's learning or access a host of beneficial opportunities for their children. The staff FET team members work closely with families to co-create a FAQ document with more than forty questions that is both texted and mailed to all Spanish-speaking families.

What Are the Goals of a FET Team?

A FET team's overarching goals are to strengthen relationships, trust, and communication between staff and traditionally marginalized families and spark collaboration that leads to meaningful change.

Strengthen Relationships and Build Trust

Fostering two-way dialogue builds relationships, explores assumptions from new angles, helps us recognize each other's humanity, and can lead to what many in the field call "solidarity-driven, shoulder to shoulder" collaboration (Bergman, 2022). Creating more equitable and just schools is "not a simple flipping of the power dynamic to put parents in control, but rather a shared and collaborative relationship between the two parties" (Mapp et al., 2022, pp. 90–91). This collaborative relationship is one of the most important overarching goals of FET.

When researchers studied the schools that were positive outliers during the first two years of the COVID-19 pandemic, a common thread between them was strong relationships (Kamenetz, 2022). When Mapp and colleagues (2022) looked closely at these schools, they found that educators "viewed relationship-building with families as the fundamental first step in establishing a positive culture at the school and ensuring student success" (p. 58). Positive changes and genuine reforms cannot begin until families have enough relational trust to feel safe in speaking their truths (Winthrop, 2022).

The schools that accelerate their trust-building efforts are—not coincidentally—the same schools that make tremendous progress around their goals (Tschannen-Moran, 2014). When researchers studied the characteristics of thirty high-performing schools compared with thirty low-performing schools in Chicago, they discovered that teachers in the high-performing schools reported higher levels of trust with one another *and* with parents (Payne, 2008).

When I spoke with Marta Loachamin, the mother of a former student, months before she successfully pursued her race to become a county commissioner, Marta told me that she recently had completed dozens of focus groups with underrepresented families around their experiences in all sectors of society. Looking back on her conversations with parents, Marta told me that, going into the project, "Our hypothesis was that language would be the greatest barrier. In the end, we learned that trust was actually the largest barrier" (M. Loachamin, personal communication, April 16, 2019).

Collaborate to Effect Meaningful Change

Once we have developed sufficient trust and a shared understanding of the team's purpose, we can shift to action. Through collaborating on tangible steps that foster positive change, all participants in FET deepen their sense of personal and collective efficacy. When good ideas for creating positive change emerge at schools without teams, it is hard to implement them in isolation. They need to be part of a comprehensive, ongoing, and systemic approach (Epstein & Associates, 2018). As Hong (2019) writes, "We need strategies that seek to build cultural change *within* schools" (p. 13). FET teams provide this practical and replicable forum to achieve these types of changes.

Since FET is not a concept that most families or educators are familiar with initially, we have found it is crucial to effectively communicate the overarching purposes of these teams. The following are the six FET purpose statements. Visit **go.SolutionTree.com /diversityandequity** for a free reproducible version of this list.

1. Strengthen trust-based, reciprocal relationships between school staff and underrepresented families.

2. Build stronger ties and an informal network between underrepresented families so that they feel part of a larger community and experience greater collective agency.

3. Engage in meaningful dialogue that centers the voices of marginalized family members and leads to cross-cultural learning.

4. Equip families with the information they need to navigate the school system and effectively advocate for their children's education.

5. Help educators discover more effective approaches to fostering connection and understanding the experiences of culturally and linguistically diverse families.

6. Codesign transformative action projects that remove barriers and lead to more collaborative and equitable school communities.

> In the middle of their first year as a FET team, the team leaders at New Vista High School asked the families, "Do you feel clear on the purpose of this team? Is it meeting your needs?"
>
> One of the mothers on the team spoke up immediately. She had spent the previous four years participating on the FET teams at her children's elementary and middle schools.
>
> "FET has been so helpful. The team builds strong relationships between the team leaders and the families so that we have someone we can go to for support. It has improved communication and given us access to the principal. I've seen how it helps the teachers better understand our barriers as Latinos and the language challenges that we experience. We're no longer as lost in terms of all the information the schools send us. As parents, we share our needs, and you share yours, which makes it very reciprocal. Our families now participate more at school. I've learned so much at FET and grown in so many ways. We're also more connected as a community."

How Did FET Meetings Evolve?

When I assumed district leadership of the FET initiative in its second year, I was inspired by its driving purpose. I was also deeply grateful to my predecessor, Madeline Case, for both her initiative and vision in launching pilot teams at six different schools. She wisely observed that "there was a lot of energy around wanting to cultivate partnerships between families and educators, but a lot of times there weren't clear goals, strategies, and focus to the work" (Eakins, n.d.). Madeline recognized that schools needed a structure where they could focus on relationships and "changing school cultures so that they are welcoming and value families." As she recalls, "FET was loosely based on the National Network for Partnership Schools with a lot of our own twists" (Eakins, n.d.).

In working with the initial six schools during their second year of FET, it quickly became apparent to me that we needed to clearly define what an optimal meeting looked like, for both team leaders and participants. While teams usually built in time for quick introductions, they tended to jump immediately into conversations that were often not outcome oriented or focused on a clear topic for the remainder of the meeting. There was no consistent structure either for individual teams or across all FET teams.

At many sites, despite the intention to prioritize parent voices, teachers and principals fell into the familiar pattern of doing the lion's share of the talking. Another factor hampering trust building was the group's physical configuration. Often, families were seated in one part of the room and educators in another. At times, some participants were hidden behind others, or they were put in clusters of small tables even though most of the meeting required whole-group conversation. Team leaders were often set apart from the group. It did not feel like one solid team.

To better meet the goals of FET, we leaned heavily on what I'd learned from my decade of experience training teachers and school leaders how to create engaging classrooms at Passageworks Institute (Weaver & Wilding, 2013). While this work gave us a bank of team-building activities and conversation structures to draw upon in FET, the way we engaged adult learners was the most vital gift from these experiences. Participants in these Passageworks trainings came from various schools. Most did not know anyone else on Friday afternoon when we started. However, by mid-Saturday morning, the level of connection and cohesion left me awestruck.

As I learned in my years of training others and after testing many approaches, I have found eight SEL and equity-centered facilitator practices consistently cultivate high levels of engagement and a strong sense of community for any group of adults. Those eight are as follows.

1. Carve out ample time for planning in the weeks leading up to the gathering.

2. Sequence the agenda so that it contains the right activities in a familiar order, making it easy for participants to bring their full selves, maximize engagement, and accelerate group cohesion.

3. Engage early on in team-building activities so that people feel the joy of community in an embodied way and feel connected to others before they are asked to speak.

4. Use equity-based talk structures (see appendix D, page 147, for a detailed list) that ensure participants have equal time to share and strengthen their capacities for deep listening and authentic speaking.

5. Bring in everyone's voice early and often and with great intentionality. Start with each person sharing their name and some surface-level personal information. Then, support greater confidence by asking them to converse with various partners around engaging prompts. Finally, have them share in the larger group once they feel connected to many individuals.

6. Pose meaningful questions, such as those found in appendix D (page 147), that resonate with everyone for whole-group sharing. As people feel increasingly safer being more vulnerable, use prompts that probe greater depths.

7. Trust the agenda but be willing to pivot in real time based on what is unfolding in the group.

8. Model authenticity, curiosity, and other qualities that you would like participants to embody.

While these practices were effective with teachers and school leaders at the Passageworks trainings, I wondered if they would work as well with parents. Would it be as applicable in groups like FET that were more diverse in terms of language, culture, and national origin? Despite the fact that when we enter our first FET meeting, educators typically represent the traditionally dominant group in terms of race, class, language, and positional power, could this approach effectively level the playing field so that every voice was equally valued? Would it support the educators who enter their first meeting with their guards up and often feel tentative, or family members who wonder if this will be yet another school gathering where teachers talk to or at them?

Overall, the answer to whether these SEL and equity-centered facilitator practices would work with parents has been a resounding *yes*. We now use these eight principles to guide our FET gatherings. By the time we leave the first FET meeting, everyone can feel that this is a unique space where team building is prioritized and everyone's voice is valued. Regardless of the age or background of participants, our most authentic selves are unleashed and groups flourish when there are high levels of trust and people feel deeply connected to each other (Tschannen-Moran, 2014).

How Does FET Compare to Other Kinds of Partnership Teams?

FET is similar to other school-based and parent-centered entities such as PTA and School Accountability Committee (SAC) in that it focuses on parent participation and input that ultimately benefits all students in a school community. Like PTA, SAC, and other committees that center parent voices, FET is ultimately focused on school improvement.

However, the focus and composition of a FET team is significantly different from your typical SAC or PTA. A SAC team usually contains more staff participants than family members. Rather than focusing on families' experiences within the school or those of their children, SAC is an advisory team that primarily focuses on reviewing school budgets and academic data, and to a lesser degree focuses on discussing family engagement. SAC members report to the principal, and the agendas of meetings are driven by staff needs and priorities.

In the dozens of schools I have worked in or worked with, the overarching focus of the PTA or PTO (parent-teacher organization) has been fundraising and coordinating events for students and families. While participating parents share their thoughts about what transpires at school, the PTA's priority is not centered on how to improve the school community for underrepresented students and families or to support educators in partnering more effectively with families. Additionally, immigrant families or parents of color do not typically comprise the majority of parents within a school's PTA, and the language used in meetings is predominantly English. Alongside the school principal, there is usually just one staff representative at each PTA meeting.

In addition to SAC and PTA, some districts have parent groups or committees that are focused on underrepresented families. Some of these are district-based entities that perform an advisory role for a superintendent, which often means the goals and topics of conversation are driven by district employees rather than families. In other instances, these committees are school-based, and their primary aim is to create an affinity space where parents of a particular cultural or linguistic background can build bonds among themselves while supporting the school with event coordination.

FET is different from these entities in a host of ways. As we have already explored, the heart of a FET team's efforts is cultivating stronger relationships and mutual learning between staff and underrepresented families. FET teams include several staff members rather than a single representative, and meetings are usually conducted in the language spoken by most of the FET team families. Unlike these other parent-based organizations, discussions spring from the needs of the parents.

FET is focused on steadily co-creating a more cohesive and equitable school, eradicating barriers, and transforming existing practices. When I asked one of our teacher leaders who serves on her school's diversity, equity, and inclusion (DEI) committee how FET is different, she said, "FET is from the inside out as other groups like DEI are from the outside in. FET belongs to the members" (L. Moore, personal communication, April 10, 2023).

What Are the Four Pillars of Authentic School-Family Partnerships?

"I've had a child at this school for twelve years, and I've never felt as connected as I do tonight," a Spanish-speaking father shared at an elementary school's first FET meeting. "Tomorrow I will say hello to a teacher that I wouldn't have said hello to today."

What happened in ninety minutes to create this shift for this father and dozens of other parents? One of the roots to the answer lies in the four pillars of school-family partnerships:

1. Engaging in two-way communication
2. Cultivating relationships and trust
3. Supporting learning and social-emotional well-being
4. Sharing decision making and power

As shown in figure 1.1 (page 28), intercultural understanding is the foundation holding up these four pillars.

The four pillars are a succinct way to explicate what is meant by *authentic partnerships*. I created these four pillars in 2018, alongside colleagues from the University of Colorado Boulder. The pillars were influenced by Auerbach's (2012) research and her book *School Leadership for Authentic Family and Community Partnerships: Research Perspectives for Transforming Practice*. We created the pillars because our school district needed a conceptual framework and common language to inform our existing and future school-family partnership efforts.

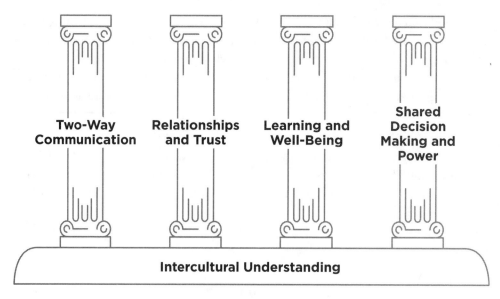

Figure 1.1: The four pillars of authentic school-family partnerships.

The other reason we created this framework was because at the time the PTA national standards felt too oriented toward a White, middle- to upper-class demographic. As I write this in the spring of 2023, the PTA has released more culturally responsive standards, but in 2018 a standard such as "communicating effectively" did not fully address linguistic, cultural, and other barriers that made pathways to two-way communication so vital for our families (Mapp et al., 2022). In addition, the continued marginalization of many of our immigrant families and parents of color meant that we as educators needed to develop greater intercultural understanding and prioritize cultivating trusting relationships for any other outcomes to be achieved.

The relationships formed at a first FET gathering and the growing communication about parents' interests and needs incorporate the first two pillars: two-way communication, and relationships and trust. Stronger relationships and higher levels of trust are essential before families and educators can speak honestly or create effective change (Tschannen-Moran, 2014). As Stephen Covey's (2008) research into highly effective organizations reveals, change happens at the speed of trust, and trust moves at the speed of relationship.

Shared decision making also begins to happen. As Auerbach (2012) writes, "Sharing power in socially just schools means inviting stakeholders to the table as full partners, working in coalition with them, and empowering them to share leadership" (pp. 37–38). Additionally, exploring topics that families are interested in learning more about at future meetings makes it clear both families' and students' learning and well-being are valued. Intercultural understanding is the foundation holding up these four pillars. We cannot identify solutions until we generate a deeper understanding of the families themselves and the systems that maintain the inequities we are aiming to transform (Ishimaru, 2020).

To honor these four pillars, and to move from the family involvement model that has dominated most schools' family outreach efforts, our district made critical shifts. We began focusing on how participating parents *feel* more than on what they *do* at gatherings so process would take priority over content. Asking families what they need (instead of guessing) and incorporating time in gatherings to *listen to* families and facilitate interactions, rather than *talking to* them, was another significant change. We also tried to value all the ways that families can support their children's learning at home, rather than focusing on attendance at events as the main measure of involvement.

Conclusion

So far, we have explored the essence of FET: what it is and who participates, its purpose, and what distinguishes it from other parent-centered teams. Every FET team is different, but to summarize what we have covered, the key goals they need to achieve are the same.

- Create a trusting space for historically marginalized families to share their experiences.
- Help educators reshape the ways they foster connection and understand the experiences of culturally and linguistically diverse parents.
- Design meaningful gatherings and demonstrate consistent follow-through amid competing time pressures and the inherently challenging role of parent or educator.
- Create a sense of unity amid cultural, linguistic, and power differences.
- Deepen the level of trust while accomplishing measurable change that creates a more collaborative and just school.

In the next chapter, we will take a detailed look at who makes up a FET team, and how to assemble a team.

Questions for Reflection and Discussion

1. How is your school currently partnering with underrepresented families or making space for their voices to be heard?
2. What aspects of the purpose and goals of FET most resonate with you?
3. When you think about forging a FET team, which families would likely be the primary audience in your school or district? Which colleagues would most likely join you in launching this effort?
4. As you reflect on the family involvement versus authentic partnerships chart (table I.1, page 7), in what ways are you currently demonstrating an involvement or a partnerships approach? Overall, where is your school or district on this continuum?
5. What are the greatest barriers for you or your school to forging deeper partnerships with families?

CHAPTER 2

Building Your Teams

Both families and educators have expertise we need in order to "fix" our systems—and both need to build capacity to work toward systemic change.

—Ann Ishimaru

For schools to strengthen partnerships with families consistently, effectively, and meaningfully, we must move beyond isolated events and random interactions and instead rely on the ongoing structure of collaborative teams. To create a high-trust environment for nondominant families and school staff to tackle structural inequities and disrupt the status quo requires a sturdy foundation from the very beginning.

Bringing educators and families together effectively requires building teams, and that is an art. School districts and schools have many teams, but very few of them include families, and even fewer contain both families and educators. For such a team to harness meaningful change and be genuinely collaborative, it also needs the right people, purpose, resources, and structure. Building a team across cultural, linguistic, and power differences also requires a particular level of thoughtfulness.

In this chapter, we will explore the responsibilities and recruitment of FET team members, the importance of having a district lead, and the qualities of excellent team leaders.

Define FET Team Roles

Most of the tasks of planning and leading FET gatherings will fall to the team leaders. While the principal plays a vital role in communicating with staff and collaborating with team leaders to carry out FET action projects, the principal's primary role at meetings is to listen and strengthen relationships with families. There are many roles played on a FET team that contribute to an effective meeting, and it's important that the team leaders delegate some of these to their colleagues on the team. The most important supportive roles for team members to take on include:

- Premeeting greeter
- Person to pick up meal if it is not being delivered
- Notetaker
- Participant tracker
- Timekeeper
- Small-group reporters
- Spokesperson to summarize and share out with rest of school staff
- Spokesperson to summarize and share out with families

A premeeting greeter can help team members feel welcome, especially if it's their first meeting. Having someone in this role also provides an initial point of contact if an arrival has questions and can help direct attendees to the meeting room. As we will discuss more later, providing a meal is a central part of FET meetings. Delegating someone in advance who is responsible for making sure the food arrives can be especially helpful.

It is important to capture good notes of the night's discussion. In addition to a notetaker, a team leader will typically write team members' ideas on chart paper during discussion, which helps team members feel that their voices are valued and can drive the team's work forward. As such, it is important to decide who will take notes and chart for the meeting. Similarly, it can be helpful to track how often team members contribute, a task that could potentially be done by the notetaker or someone in another of these roles.

Another role that can be helpful is a timekeeper. While meetings should feel informal and responsive to the needs and interests of the group (particularly the family members), it can be helpful to have someone keep a regular eye on the clock so you have time to determine next steps and engage in meaningful closure before the gathering ends.

Small-group reporters can be arranged in advance or as team members divide into groups. Having a designated person to report on the group's discussion can help ensure that all significant points are recorded and can then be referenced later.

While there may be other roles that you decide would be helpful to meet the unique needs of your team, the last I will recommend here is that of a spokesperson for the FET team. This team member (or members) is tasked with the responsibility of ensuring that the greater school and family community is aware of FET team discussion topics and happenings. It can be helpful to have a separate spokesperson for the staff and for the families.

Which Staff Members Participate on the Team?

All school staff members are welcome to participate on the team. As FET has grown in strength and popularity in my district, several principals have made it an official committee, which has led some staff members to voluntarily sign up and attend all monthly gatherings. In other schools, team leaders and administrators may identify colleagues who would potentially be interested in joining the team and informally recruit them. While the fact that FET gatherings occur in the evening may be a deterrent for staff who have young children or live a significant distance from the school, many consider FET their favorite school gathering. They are drawn to the opportunity to deepen relationships and learn from families, as well as a delicious and free dinner. At many schools, principals have established FET as one of the committees that staff are asked to participate in, and occasionally, budget permitting, schools may offer a stipend to staff who participate on the team.

While all staff are welcome to join the team, there are several roles that merit top consideration. It is essential that either the principal or an assistant principal attend every gathering. Since FET typically centers on English-learner families, it is important to prioritize the staff who work most closely with the families of emerging bilinguals, such as the family liaison, the English language development teacher, or the newcomer teacher at schools that have this position. Ideally, the school counselor or someone in a similar student-support position participates on the team. At elementary schools, preferably there is representation from a variety of grade-level teams. At middle and high schools, it is ideal to have someone from most departments.

The aim is to have at least five educators on the team, including the team leaders and principal in attendance. In addition to this core set of staff members is an open invitation to their colleagues to join once or twice in the first half of the year and then return as often as they would like. Time and again, I have seen that when a larger percentage of staff attends at least one gathering throughout the year, it leads families to feel like they have more staff that they know and can trust. What has been even more intriguing is that FET families tend to extend that trust more generously to staff members that they have never met.

For the initial meetings, it is difficult to predict how many families will join. Consequently, to help families feel more comfortable, it is preferable to have fewer staff members to ensure that there are more parents present than educators. Once the team has gained momentum by the second or third month, it is great to incorporate additional staff members, as long as they don't outnumber the parents.

FET teams do not flourish if the principal is not committed to attending each meeting and invested in supporting the team to succeed. The steady involvement of the principal conveys to families that their participation and voice matter. Administrators' presence at these night gatherings lets staff know that this collaboration with underrepresented families is a valued priority rather than a committee on the margins of the school.

Which Families Participate on the Team?

Since the beginning of FET in 2016, the target audience has usually been Latino families, as their children comprise 20 percent of our district's student population and are represented at considerably higher levels at several of our schools. Of the more than twenty-five schools that have participated in FET, fifteen teams have focused entirely on involving Latino families and use Spanish as the language of each gathering, whereas the other ten have included immigrant families from a diverse array of countries, as well as parents of color born in the United States.

A new team's leaders should have a thorough conversation about which families they are most interested in recruiting so the team can be clear and focused in its outreach efforts. Although one of the aims of FET is to ultimately support all families who have been traditionally marginalized, the decision to focus on the most prominent underrepresented families is a practical and strategic one, and not intended to exclude potential families who might participate. As renowned facilitator Priya Parker (2018) writes, "I have learned that far too often in the name of inclusion and generosity—two values that I care about deeply—we fail to draw boundaries about who belongs and why" (p. 38).

It cannot be overstated how important it has been for many students' families in my school district that Spanish be the language of our gathering. It automatically disrupts the power imbalance between educators and families and leads participating parents to feel more comfortable, confident, and valued. As one parent put it at our inaugural FET Parent Leadership Summit, "FET helps us feel like we belong. We can speak and be heard in our language around any problem or need that we have as Latinos. They take us into account."

For this reason, in schools where we know that Spanish-speaking families would naturally comprise 80 percent or more of the family representatives, we have only been able to include families who speak languages other than English and Spanish at home if they are proficient enough to benefit from the English interpretation provided at every meeting. We simply cannot find interpreters that are able to traverse, for instance, a Spanish to Turkish interpretation or Spanish to Korean need.

Schools can take other steps to ensure these underrepresented families feel seen, heard, and more integrated into the school community through such best practices as home visits or occasionally hosting a gathering in their specific language (for example, Nepali). This remains a growth edge for many of our schools. However, a handful of existing FET schools serve as a model for how to form highly effective and cohesive multilingual and multicultural teams.

Let's take a brief look at Fireside Elementary as one example. As our discussions began around forming a FET team, it was clear that based on the shifting demographics of the school, we were aiming to have an international team and only a small number of participants would hail from Spanish-speaking countries. During the team's first year, we had participating parents who were born in Israel, Japan, El Salvador, Mali, Bosnia, Mexico, and Thailand. We made a clear and somewhat easy decision in the month preceding the first meeting that we would host the gatherings in English and have interpreters present for any languages that families requested.

As far as who else participates on FET teams, if there is a district leader who coordinates and supports FET teams, they should attend all the monthly meetings of schools in their first year of having a FET team, and ideally teams with new team leaders. At some schools, a community leader or two might attend meetings. They can offer insights from their vantage points and learn from the perspectives of both families and educators.

Students can also bring valuable perspectives to FET. Elementary students can attend a portion of FET gatherings to present to the team or join the playful team-building activities. At the middle and high school levels, one or more students might join the conversation regularly. Their presence can consistently enrich the conversation as they either bring forth issues or perspectives that other stakeholders can't see or provide valuable insight when team members bring up a topic and need more concrete examples from the trenches.

Designate a District Lead

Many individual schools can use this book as a guide to successfully implement a FET team in the absence of a district-level leader. However, all of us who have been school-based educators know that we are typically in a state of overwhelm. This limits our capacity to launch new initiatives, particularly if we have minimal training in that realm.

One of the reasons that the FET structure consistently thrives across a cross section of schools is because it is led by leaders from the staff and community, and not a school leader such as a principal or assistant principal. This ensures from the beginning that the team is not top-down and unduly influenced by the positional power of the principal, with parents and staff treading lightly or regularly deferring to the principal's vision.

Unfortunately, principals and other school leaders have such a plethora of responsibilities that they usually lack the bandwidth to provide the level of support that team leaders need to be successful. Particularly in the first year (or each time there is turnover in the leadership of the FET team), team leaders need ample support, on everything from recruiting staff to guidance on executing the key logistics that help teams flourish to how to be an effective facilitator. Additionally, very few principals have been trained in school-family partnership best practices, facilitation skills, or culturally responsive strategies for leading teams with families whose backgrounds are different from their own.

All this is to say that it can be extremely beneficial to have a district lead coordinating the effort. Many districts have a designated position with the word *family* in that person's professional title, such as a family partnerships director or family outreach liaison. For those districts that still lack this position, they likely have director or cabinet-level positions focused on community engagement, Title I schools, English language development, or equity. Any one of these individuals can be the point person for coordinating the FET effort. Ideally, the chosen individual would have a passion for improving school-family partnerships and strengthening cross-cultural skills, as well as the ability to both effectively facilitate and coach others to do so.

If it is not possible to have a district lead play this vital support role, it can be done by a principal or teacher leader. Throughout this book, I will be referring to this FET team coordinator as the district lead, but this role can be fulfilled by other leaders as well. Once this district lead is selected, it is important that FET be placed near the top of their priority list and is not one of dozens of responsibilities on their plate.

If you are striving to identify and recruit a district-level colleague to take the lead with FET, you ideally want to find someone who is passionate about strengthening partnerships with underrepresented families and demonstrates a strong level of cultural responsiveness (and ideally is bilingual or multilingual). It would also be optimal to identify a district lead who is an effective communicator, builds rapport quickly, demonstrates high levels of reliability and follow-through, and would be likely to prioritize FET within their existing role. They need adequate time to devote to FET so that they can be integrally involved not only in the planning and launching phases but also in at least the entire first year of each team's journey. They will train team leads, devise agendas, cofacilitate initial meetings, troubleshoot challenges, celebrate successes, and ensure team leaders demonstrate strong follow-through.

Additionally, the district lead will provide support for a host of other logistics, such as:

- Helping with outreach efforts to families at schools that lack bilingual team leaders
- Securing childcare systemwide
- Bringing team leaders together several times a year to learn from each other
- Working closely with school leaders to solicit their interest and keep them integrally involved
- Advocating for funds to ensure that teams receive their budget and team leaders receive stipends
- Engaging in other efforts that turn FET into a firmly rooted network and intentional movement across a district, rather than the isolated effort of one or two schools that happen to have a school leader or staff member passionate about strengthening partnerships

Garner Strong Buy-In From Principals

While I have built strong, trusting relationships with many school leaders, I know as a former principal and assistant principal that school leaders wisely encounter district initiatives and "new opportunities" with healthy skepticism. They also trust the experiences and recommendations of their peers—fellow principals—over even the most sincere, well-intentioned district representatives. For this reason, I regularly encourage principals of schools with prospective FET teams to ask other principals about their experiences with FET. They will likely hear how worthwhile and meaningful it is to have a FET team, and that the rewards will far exceed the demands on both them and their participating staff members.

To ensure there is ample time to identify and onboard team leaders and avoid the end-of-the-year rush of the final month of the school year, it is ideal for the district leader or whomever will be initiating the FET team to meet with the principal or principals in April to explore whether they want to move forward in launching a FET team. While it's preferable to start team meetings in September and use the arc of the school year to gain momentum, they can launch at other times as well. FET teams continue every year and organically evolve to be responsive to the needs of families as well as staff.

In trying to convince a principal of FET's worth, aim to strike the right balance between activating their hearts and convincing their minds. You can share with them stories, anecdotes, or examples of action projects from this book, as well as some of the research on the benefits of creating a team as a vehicle for steadily strengthening partnerships. You may also share other uplifting examples with them of what parent or staff participants have said in FET gatherings and several concrete examples of change efforts that other teams have accomplished. Make sure to address the nuts and bolts as well, knowing that principals are always considerate about the impact new initiatives will have on their staff's time and bandwidth.

While you should of course have notes and stories prepared in advance, let their questions guide the conversation so that it's engaging and it doesn't seem like a sales pitch. Tell them just enough so there aren't any big gaps in their understanding of FET but not so much that they feel overwhelmed. Considering how crucial their belief in FET is for it to succeed, it's important to let them decide if they are going to start a team or not. A principal may respond with something along the lines of "It is so helpful to have a better understanding of what FET is. I don't think that the time is ripe to start next fall, but a year from then would be perfect, and I'd like to partner with you next year to lay a foundation for the staff."

When a principal does express interest in launching a team, the next move is to hold a half-hour gathering with the entire school staff at a faculty meeting. Approach this meeting like the principal conversation and stay primarily focused on the purpose of FET, inspiring examples or research, and your school's unique communication needs.

Principals will continue to have a role in FET even after they have granted approval. One of the core reasons that FET teams flourish is because school leaders are consistently involved and devoted to the work. Principals' attendance at FET meetings is essential for four main reasons.

1. Families become more confident when they feel familiar with the principal, know that leader on a first name basis, and see them as accessible.

2. The team's change efforts can be implemented more easily and effectively if the principal has the context and has been a part of the ongoing conversations.

3. When staff see that the principal carves out time to attend FET meetings, they are more likely to participate and feel valued in doing so.

4. The principal learns a tremendous amount by listening to families' perspectives and grows their and the school's capacity to better partner with all families.

While school leaders primarily listen in FET meetings and play a support role to their team leaders, their presence, genuine investment in the vision of FET, and behind-the-scenes support are absolutely vital (Epstein & Associates, 2018).

Jones Middle School had the largest population of Latino students and families of all our district's middle schools at the time. Unfortunately, the principal did not attend FET gatherings. He had assigned the community liaison and front office secretary to lead the team. They were not interested in spending time planning a detailed agenda. Additionally, they did not communicate consistently with families and staff about upcoming meetings, and as a result turnout was often low. They also held meetings at 8:30 in the morning to accommodate what worked for staff, but this time proved challenging for most families who were interested in attending.

Things reached a nadir midyear when I arrived for a meeting and neither team leader showed up to facilitate the gathering. The three teachers and one parent in attendance could tell that the team leaders were not committed. When I approached the principal about this latest misstep, he quickly became defensive and told me that the district could have its money back, referring to the small budget supporting the team's efforts.

While I was subsequently able to get buy-in for shifting to after-school gatherings and greater commitment to the planning process, I sensed that the principal and two team leaders did not have their hearts in the effort. It was clear also that they were not truly interested in sharing power with families. While participating staff spoke regularly of the chasm between them and most Latino families, the school leader's lack of commitment and participation led to the sad but inevitable move in May to disband the team. The principal left the district in 2020, and in 2023 we relaunched a FET team at Jones.

Fortunately, the experience at Jones positively informed the launch of all subsequent FET teams as it led me to be intentional in conveying to principals how crucial their presence and support is for the ultimate success of their team. It also provided clarity that a school should not launch a FET team until their principal is enthusiastic and ready to take on this additional commitment. Additionally, since those challenges with lackluster principal involvement at Jones and a couple other schools in the early years of FET, principals have been remarkably devoted, passionate, and grateful to have a team at their school.

Identify and Recruit Team Leaders

Once there is strong buy-in from the principal and staff are aware of FET and the intention to launch a team, the next critical step is to identify between two and five teachers and parents who will co-lead the team. Selecting team leaders is one of the most important and consequential choices in forming a new team.

The principal will likely be able to identify two to five prospective leaders. Staff members who are champions of school-family partnerships and embody the qualities of a strong team leader should also be given top consideration. Consider consulting with a colleague (or two) who is a veteran at the school; their insights may inform the selection process. At times, the staff member who first learns about FET and works to initiate a team is an ideal candidate to serve as one of the team leaders. One of the most effective ways to solicit strong candidates is for the principal—after the initial overview presentation about FET is given to the whole staff—to ask who is interested and then select the candidates that best match the attributes of a great team leader defined in the next section of this chapter (page 40).

Recruiting family members to serve as team leaders typically happens at the end of a FET team's first year once the principal and initial team leaders have had the opportunity to see who are the most passionate, relational, and consistent in their participation. Regardless of when family members come aboard as new team leaders, we have found that the best candidates are those who are highly reliable, have great people and communications skills, are dedicated to the mission of FET, and are both comfortable collaborating with educators and well respected by other parents. While we tend to schedule our planning sessions around what is convenient for the parent leaders on a team, it is also helpful if they are flexible and can be counted on to attend trainings, leadership gatherings, planning sessions, and team meetings. While it might seem like a natural choice to have a family or community liaison be one of the team leaders (and this has been the case at some schools with FET teams), it is important to keep in mind that another benefit of FET is cultivating other staff members who can serve as bridges between the school and families, a role that liaisons already effectively play.

Once the new team leaders have been identified, it's best to personalize the onboarding conversation and meet one-on-one or one-on-two with each new leader. Particularly when a district leader is coordinating the launch of the FET team, it is valuable for them to forge a solid relationship with new team leaders from day one and recognize that for them to succeed, they need information and inspiration from the start. This approach is in alignment with the spirit of FET, which at its core is about building stronger relationships and higher levels of trust one conversation at a time. Also, it can be beneficial to encourage new team leaders to attend a FET meeting at another school, if that's an option, to observe the meeting structure and facilitation.

There are no prescribed limits to the years that leaders can serve. On average, team leaders serve for two full school years. Since you will want to keep strong leaders on board for as long as possible, ask existing team leaders to let you know if they are resigning from their position ideally two months before the end of the school year so there is ample time to recruit a replacement leader.

Not just any educator or family member can be an effective team leader. Among other capacities, they need to be reliable and demonstrate strong follow-through, have passion for working closely with families, and be comfortable leading a diverse group of families and educators. Creating an engaging space that allows families and educators to show up authentically requires both thoughtful planning and strong facilitation moves.

While FET team leaders likely possess skill and passion for the work, they may have minimal experience facilitating meetings. They likely have not led groups of adults or had extensive training in school-family best practices. Ideally, they are educators and parents who are open to new learning and receptive to well-intentioned coaching, particularly around facilitation skills and creating engaging and meaningful gatherings. In my experience, I have seen just how much of the success of the FET team hinges on team leaders' effectiveness from moment to moment in each monthly meeting.

Know the Qualities of Great Team Leaders

There are certainly a handful of qualities and skills that greatly support successful FET leadership. Overall, FET leaders are most effective when all team members feel comfortable during meetings, safe enough to share honestly, and valued enough that they want to continue participating on the team.

While some initial discomfort or nervousness for all team members is to be expected, it is vital that FET leaders reduce participants' anxiety, reluctance to participate, or disinterest in returning for future meetings. When I reflect on the team leaders who accomplish this most effectively, they possess a sense of authenticity, a natural rapport with others, and an attunement to the mood, goals, and well-being of the team as a whole.

Be Authentic

The most successful FET team leaders are comfortable in their own skin and fully inhabit themselves—their physicality, their words, their emotions. By showing up with humility and vulnerability, they make it easier for others to put down their guards and do the same. The author and educator Angeles Arrien (2001) calls this type of leader a *visionary*, someone who "brings his or her voice into the world and refuses to edit, rehearse, perform, or hide" and recognizes that "the power of creativity is aligned with authenticity" (p. 151).

Additionally, strong team leaders have high levels of self-awareness. For instance, they are attuned to the fact that most communication is nonverbal (Michail, 2020) and optimize their impact by communicating nonverbally in welcoming ways. They avoid talking too much and speak clearly, directly, and succinctly. Often, these leaders exhibit a good sense of humor and regularly weave in moments of levity.

Finally, strong team leaders garner trust from team members through their integrity, which emerges when they show respect, keep their word, are honest about mistakes they make, and are transparent about not possessing all the answers. As Fullan (2011) writes, "Leaders who thrive and survive are people who know they don't know everything. In fact this knowledge—knowing that you don't know—is crucial for enabling others" (p. 126).

Build Rapport

First and foremost, strong FET leaders help others feel valued and safe by listening well and showing that they are focused on the needs and interests of others (Knight, 2022). They pay attention to what has heart and meaning (Lantieri, 2001).

Effective FET leaders are also gifted at building relationships with a diverse array of individuals. They show a sensitivity and knack for building rapport with others, often across linguistic and cultural differences, which makes them approachable and accessible. One of the ways they achieve this is by front-loading relationship building. They reach out to families between meetings via text or phone calls and use those opportunities to build relationships. Additionally, they use the time before and after meetings to make individual connections and foster trust with participants.

They are also cross-cultural ambassadors. How do they accomplish this feat? Among other things, they demonstrate a genuine curiosity about other people's experiences and an openness to their ideas. Exemplary leaders also uncover and recognize the strengths of others and regularly show an appreciation for cultural assets (Krownapple, 2017). Finally, they navigate differences with poise and respect.

Attune to the Whole Team

Great FET leaders also facilitate in ways that show attunement with the well-being of the whole team and not just each individual. By this, I mean that they put people first yet also stay focused on efficiency, progress, measurable goals, and clearly defined outcomes, an approach that Megan Tschannen-Moran (2014) calls "soft on people and tough on projects" (p. 188). They also propel the team forward through these additional approaches:

- Tracking who is speaking and who is not, and finding subtle ways to encourage balanced participation
- Exhibiting patience in moments of group incoherence
- Demonstrating courage and, at times, fearlessness to ask tough questions or raise uncomfortable truths
- Remaining comfortable and composed as difficult emotions surface
- Taking risks in order to strengthen connections
- Approaching gatherings with a clarity of purpose *and* the flexibility to be responsive and spontaneous when it serves the group

This list captures what I have learned from both the successes and missteps of the approximately 150 FET leaders that I have had the privilege to work with since 2017.

Conclusion

This chapter introduced FET team roles and how to put together a FET team. It also explored the significance and qualities of great team leaders, and the critical role both principals and team leaders play in the success of any FET team.

Teams thrive when the district lead lays out an inspiring vision, immediately focuses on building trustful relationships, and ensures that logistics are effectively addressed. In the next chapter, we will look at the steps teams take in the opening weeks of the school year to ensure a strong first FET meeting.

Questions for Reflection and Discussion

1. Who might be the best colleagues to lead a FET team at both the district level and school level?

2. Which underrepresented families do you want to prioritize as you prepare to launch a team?

3. What were your biggest takeaways in terms of how to elicit strong buy-in from your principal or district leadership?

4. How will you efficiently and effectively recruit colleagues to join the team? Who can help you in this endeavor, and what information about FET do you think will be most compelling to share with prospective team members?

5. Of the many optimal team leader qualities you read about, which most surprised you, and why?

CHAPTER 3

Preparing for the Launch

Diligence is the mother of good fortune.

—Miguel de Cervantes

One of the most crucial things I've learned after half-a-dozen years of leading FET is the importance of *preparation*. If staff members, team leaders, and principals feel well informed and invested in starting a FET team, it bolsters their capacity in the opening month of the school year for the hard work of preparing for a successful first meeting.

When FET teams take specific steps in the spring to establish the groundwork, they are more likely to thrive in the fall. This window of time is vital for laying the groundwork for a successful launch of a FET team, but it is competing with many other pressing responsibilities on everyone's time. As a result, it is essential that we are strategic, intentional, and efficient in our efforts to build the foundation for a strong first gathering.

The first month of the school year is intense for *all* stakeholders. Ideally, teams should put certain foundational pieces in place in the spring to set themselves up for success. Most importantly, the district lead, or whoever is taking on this role, should proactively reach out to connect with, enlist, onboard, and garner strong buy-in from the principal and team leaders, as well as staff members who may participate on the team.

While district leads cannot put off the various tasks that set a team up for success, it is important that they not demand too much of team leaders at such a frenzied time of the school year. They can do so by recognizing that FET is just a small sliver of an educator's professional responsibilities and a very part-time commitment for parent leaders.

Because of these time constraints, a two-hour team leader training meeting is sufficient. Any remaining key components can be embedded in monthly planning sessions. The secret to effectively using the opening weeks of the school year is to help FET leaders become crystal clear on the must-dos and why those tasks will be impactful. It is also vital to support them in scaffolding these tasks to minimize any potential overwhelm. Any vital guidance that is not highlighted in the training should be conveyed either in the first planning session or via email. If the guidance is valuable for all FET teams, it is efficient and effective to send various tips or reminders in a single email to all FET teams (see "Sample Messages From District Lead to Team Leaders" in appendix C, page 140).

In a nutshell, the three pivotal pieces for a district lead to address in the first few weeks of the school year are to tackle several logistical tasks, including training new leaders, establishing a budget and handling other early planning tasks, and maximizing recruitment efforts.

Train Team Leaders

In the days before the school year commences, bring together your new FET leaders for a two-hour training to ensure that they have a solid foundation as they begin guiding their teams. It typically makes sense to gather in the morning one or two days before their first official day because it becomes more challenging to bring everyone together once the school year has commenced. For any teacher or parent leader who cannot attend, schedule smaller make-up trainings so that every new FET leader has been trained before they begin planning and leading meetings. Ensure every new leader is trained prior to facilitating their first team meeting.

Start the training with team-builder activities to spark joy and connection, as well as to give FET leaders a sense of the value of these brief activities in positively shifting both individual and collective energy. Engaging in a few team-builders sprinkled throughout the training also gives team leaders the familiarity and confidence to lead these activities with their own FET team.

To tap into the passion and sense of purpose that inspires both educators and families to become FET leaders, "start with why," as Simon Sinek (2011) phrases it, and give each new leader an opportunity to briefly share what drew them to take on this new role. Then briefly unpack the FET purpose statements (page 23) and discuss the link between FET and the four pillars of school-family partnerships (page 27). To deepen their sense of what FET means for families, each participant could read aloud a quote from this book or from another FET meeting that comes directly from parents' reflections on the significance of FET for them and their family. By exploring the purpose statement and listening to parent voices that bring those principles to life, new leaders develop a stronger sense of what they will try to accomplish with their teams.

Remind team leaders that they shouldn't feel pressured to jump right into talking about the team's goals. Instead, encourage them to prioritize in the initial gatherings relationship building, cultivating a sense of team unity, and making it easy for every team member to participate. You'll also want to discuss the final purpose statement, which is creating actionable change efforts. Explain that those naturally unfold through the purposeful questions and dialogue that occur in early FET meetings.

Before a brief break at the halfway point, ask participants to read the elements of an effective FET gathering, which we will explore in chapter 4 (page 59). Spend some time discussing the rationale behind each facet of a FET gathering and talk about FET meeting agendas. This is also a good time to transition to discussing how to set up an environment of psychological safety for the team members. Team leaders can foster psychological safety both through fidelity to the agenda's structure and by embodying certain leadership traits.

You should also discuss the responsibilities of a team leader and the importance of clarifying with their co-leaders which roles will be shared and which will be assigned to a particular leader. During the final half hour of the training, the focus should be on a host of logistical pieces that will be critical as leaders prepare to launch or relaunch their teams once school begins. Among other things, touch briefly on:

- The team budget and leader stipend
- Good restaurants to potentially purchase meals from
- How to best set up and use interpreters and childcare
- How to make the most of the half hour before gatherings (see figure 4.2, page 61)
- The FET shared drive (which is great to set up for sharing documents between schools if multiple schools in your area have a FET team) and other printed resources that will be useful throughout the year
- A list of team-builders that they can draw upon for each meeting (see appendix D, page 147)
- The importance of regular communication and partnership with their principal about FET next steps
- The need to promptly determine dates for all meetings that school year so they don't encounter conflicts with other schoolwide events

While new team leaders typically have time to ask questions throughout the training, try to designate a few minutes at the end for Q&A. Conclude the training session in the same way most FET meetings conclude by going in a circle around the room and asking each leader to share one word that captures how they feel as they embark on this journey.

Now that the training sessions are behind you, it's important to turn to the meeting-planning logistics that should be addressed in the opening weeks of the school year.

Address the Logistics

It is important to scaffold many of the key logistical tasks in the first two to three weeks of the school year so that they are not done haphazardly in the week before the first FET meeting, which typically occurs in September. These foundational pieces may seem on the surface to be mundane tasks, but they play an absolutely critical role in ensuring a team's readiness.

There are several easy yet essential tasks that team leaders should accomplish in the opening weeks of the school year before they shift their energy to outreach. It is even better if some of these tasks can be accomplished the previous spring to lighten everyone's load as a new school year begins.

Set a Budget and Allocate Funds

In comparison to many other school efforts, and from a cost-to-benefit perspective, FET is relatively inexpensive. An annual budget of roughly $2,000 is sufficient for most teams. This enables them to spend roughly $220 per meeting on food, childcare, raffle prizes, or any other related items (for example, team T-shirts or a year-end celebration). Most of the FET budget will likely be needed to cover the cost of meals, whether those are from a local restaurant, a national chain, or a parent within the school community who might have a small catering business.

Another notable cost in launching a FET team is team leaders' stipends. Once the team is a few months into its first year, team leaders will typically devote two to three hours per month toward fulfilling their responsibilities, beyond time spent at the meeting. This is on top of the myriad responsibilities they hold in their actual roles in the school. For parent leaders, it is asking them not only to attend the FET gathering but also to carve out time to plan the agenda and engage in other efforts amid their busy familial or professional lives. As a result, paying team leaders a reasonable biannual stipend is the right thing to do, when possible.

In 2023, my district compensated our team leaders $400 per semester if they were one in a pair of leaders, or $265 a semester if they were one of three team leaders. Considering that most district budgets are dozens or hundreds of millions of dollars, when you calculate the combined cost of budgets and leadership stipends, the expense of having FET teams at five schools is a whopping $18,000 per year. This can either be built into the budget of one of the district departments, paid out of the school budgets themselves, pulled from district-level Title I funds, or accessed from grant funds.

In the early years of FET, we were able to partner with our district human resources department to compensate parent leaders from my departmental budget even though they were not employees. However, five years into FET's existence, upper leadership decided that we could no longer pay parent leaders because parents on other committees began to request stipends as well. Be sure to clarify these logistics early on, whether that is an established and ongoing commitment for your district or school to cover the costs, a local nonprofit to pay for them, or another creative alternative to compensation.

Save the Dates

Taking care of calendaring logistics early on can help avoid conflicts. Make sure to save these important dates.

FET Meetings

Select your meeting date—which day and time each month you will hold your FET meeting (for example, the second Thursday of the month from 6:00 to 7:30 p.m.). If you are the only school in your district with a FET team, you can simply pick the date of your first FET meeting and ask team members at that meeting to choose the best day of the week for most of the group going forward. If you are in a district with several FET teams, you will likely want to pick your date for each month of the school year so that the district lead can ensure that your team meeting date does not overlap with another team's meetings.

During my early years as the district lead, I remember how complicated it was when I allowed teams to wait to make this decision several weeks into the school year. Inevitably, two teams picked the same evening each month. Since both teams needed coaching and facilitation support, it created complications as one team ultimately had to find a different evening of the month and that had a domino effect on participants, childcare providers, and so on.

As you work to identify the best night of the month for your school, check your school's master calendar to avoid selecting a night that will overlap with other school events. Also, check for any major districtwide events that might create conflicts for team members. Do your best to review dates for the entire school year so that you don't need to change the date for a certain month on short notice because of a conflict. Additionally, try to avoid scheduling your night of the month on a date that will overlap with the holiday breaks in November, December, March, or April. If you do select, for instance, the fourth Wednesday of every month, early in the school year determine alternative dates for those vacation-impacted months so that you can share the new dates with the team. Avoid scheduling the meeting on a Friday evening, and if you choose Monday, please keep in mind that participants will benefit from a scheduled reminder both the previous week and the day before the meeting.

In the spirit of FET, it is ideal to give family members the decision-making power to determine both the day of the week and the exact time in the evening for each meeting. When families are asked at the first meeting, "Does this day and time work well for each of you?" or "What is the best day of the week and time for us to meet?" it immediately sets the tone that this is a different kind of school team that is centered on what is best for them and both symbolically and concretely gives them the power to decide. While it can be inconvenient for staff to wait around until an evening FET meeting starts or return to school after a short time at home, it is vital that the meeting time is optimal for most family members. Typically, the best start times for these ninety-minute meetings are usually 5:00, 5:30, and 6:00 p.m.

Planning Sessions

In addition to scheduling the FET meetings, you will want to schedule the planning sessions well in advance. Planning sessions are hour-long monthly conversations held typically a week after the previous FET meeting where the team leaders (and district leader if possible) gather to map out the agenda for the next team meeting and address all relevant logistics as well. The initial planning meeting should ideally take place at least two weeks before the first FET meeting to give team leaders ample time to prepare the agenda and avoid frantically trying to accomplish everything at the last minute.

From there, to prevent time conflicts or rounds of rescheduling, it behooves team leaders to share with the district lead a consistent day and hour each month that they will plan together. While it took several years for us to realize this, we have found that after the first FET meeting, the optimal planning day is roughly one week after the team meeting. Why? Your previous gathering will be fresh in mind, and you will still have roughly three weeks to prepare for your next meeting. Once you have confirmed a planning day and time that works for everyone, the district lead can send monthly calendar invites to team leaders for the entire school year.

Leadership Meetings

A highly effective way to support the learning and growth of all team leaders is to bring them together each quarter. This is especially relevant for districts that have multiple FET teams so that those team leaders can connect with and learn from others. These ninety-minute meetings can be virtual and scheduled however is most convenient. Leadership meetings typically mirror the structure of FET meetings in that they start with an energizing team-builder and an opening circle that gives everyone the opportunity to bring their voice into the room.

The district lead, or person facilitating FET, might touch upon logistics, such as new resources for team leaders to draw upon, restaurants that have or have not worked well for catering team meals, or relevant news on childcare, team budgets, and so on. They might also discuss leadership tactics or similar leader-focused issues, including challenges and solutions encountered.

Action projects should be touched on, to ensure that those are progressing as planned and that any additional needed support is being provided. In my experience in this position, I often highlight the action steps of a few teams that I think will inspire other teams. This includes providing concrete examples of how to turn larger goals into tangible change efforts. I also share my knowledge of how certain aspects of FET meetings may be becoming increasingly effective or ineffective and how best to pivot when needed.

One facet of the meeting that is important to have is small-group time. This allows team leaders to connect more personally with leaders from other schools. The facilitator may pose a few questions as a springboard, but this is a time for them to share and learn from each other's successes and challenges.

Similar to FET team gatherings, we often conclude our gatherings with a prompt that leads everyone to share a word, phrase, or sentence, such as "What I appreciate about my experience leading FET this year is . . ." or "I think one of my team's greatest priorities next year is . . ." These team leaders' meetings provide both practical value and inspiration to support all FET team leaders' future efforts.

Calendar Invitations

Once you have determined the monthly date for your FET team meetings, send out monthly calendar invites to all team meetings through the end of the school year to the entire staff and the district lead. These invites are sent to staff via the school email system and are not sent to families, who will receive the invitation through other communication mediums. Aim to accomplish this at least two weeks prior to your first team meeting. It will be helpful for staff who are not consistent team participants to have this invitation embedded in their calendar in case they decide to join on any given month.

Districtwide FET Calendar

As a final calendaring task, if there are multiple FET teams in your district, it's helpful to have a districtwide FET calendar document (see appendix B, page 127, for an example). This document will help ensure that one team's meetings do not overlap with another's. This makes it easier to secure childcare and interpretation support, as well as help families with children at multiple schools not have to choose between two school events on the same night of the month.

Additionally, a districtwide FET calendar can prevent FET team leaders, the district lead, and other team members from being double-booked on the same evening. The consequences when teams do not make these decisions in a timely manner are often stress and missed opportunities for a variety of stakeholders.

In the beginning of the 2022 school year, the leaders of one FET team were weeks past the suggested deadline for setting their monthly meeting times. As I anticipated from prior years when I was less persistent about teams selecting their date as soon as possible, the negative ripples quickly emerged.

For their September meeting, they chose the same night as another school, which meant our childcare providers could only support one school. In choosing their monthly meeting date, they had not checked when their parent-teacher conferences took place, so they rescheduled their October meeting for the same night that our monthly district committee for Latino parents occurs, and the one night per month that FET teams were asked to not hold their gatherings.

This example highlights the importance of a district lead having clear deadlines and kindly yet firmly being persistent with schools when they do not demonstrate follow-through. It illustrates the value of taking care of the calendaring logistics in the opening month of the school year so that this key element does not impede a FET team's ability to garner participation or make steady progress. It also underscores the importance of proactive communication and strong relationships and trust between the district lead and team leaders so that potential conflicts can be avoided or easily rectified.

While the task of calendaring can feel mundane, it is one of the most important logistics to accomplish. The following are a few other key tasks for both team leaders and the district lead to take care of in the opening weeks of the school year.

Prepare for Meetings

The following meeting elements will be explored in more depth in the next chapter, but it's important to consider them in the early planning stages.

Location

In consultation with school leaders or other colleagues, determine the optimal location for your team meetings. Consider the option of an outdoor space to take advantage of fall or spring weather for a few of your team's gatherings throughout the school year. Identify a consistent space inside the school building that is easy for families to find and has a warm and inviting quality, such as the school library. The space should have room for both a comfortable circle of chairs and a separate area for team members to engage in team-building activities or small-group conversations.

Interpreters

Carefully consider what language to hold meetings in and which languages you might potentially need an interpreter for. For teams that will meet in Spanish, interpreters should be secured for the monolingual English-speaking team members. Teams that meet in English should secure an interpreter for all the families that need the meeting to be interpreted into their home language.

It's important not to assume that families will need or will not need interpretation support. As you begin outreach, and again as the first meeting nears, remember to ask families whether they would like an interpreter. Ask each family whether they would like to have an interpreter support them at the first meeting, and what their preferred language is. For example, before a first meeting at Aspen Creek PK–8 School in my school district, the team leaders determined after speaking with parents that we would need interpreters for six of the seventeen parents at our initial gathering, and the languages for support would be Cantonese, Mongolian, Spanish, and Vietnamese.

It will likely be best to hire outside interpreters who do not work at the school. It pays off to have professional interpreters and enable any bilingual or multilingual staff members to participate as team members and not have to juggle interpreting with participating. Our district now covers all interpretation expenses for schools, instead of schools paying for them out of their own budget as they did prior to 2021. If your school has to pay for interpreters directly, please make sure to allot funds for this vital expense.

When a meeting is held in Spanish or another language aside from English, it's preferable for everyone who is not fully bilingual to use an interpretation headset. In my district, initially only non-Spanish speakers used headsets, and then we realized that it was more effective to have Spanish speakers briefly put on their headsets when a staff member shared in English. Doing simultaneous instead of consecutive interpretation both saved us time and supported interpreters in being able to provide a more accurate, word-for-word interpretation in the moment. Your school can either purchase a dozen or so of these headsets or request that the interpreter you hire, who will often have them, bring headsets with them.

Childcare

For parents and other family members to be able to relax and be fully present in the team meeting, childcare support is essential. As such, plan on providing childcare for families. It's possible that middle and high school teams may not need childcare, but it is best to provide it at the first meeting and ask parents if it is needed moving forward. Across the United States, it has become increasingly challenging to find consistent childcare support. Whether you are hiring professionals or drawing upon a local entity that can provide reliable and vetted volunteers, work to secure this support as soon as possible.

Depending on your school's needs, the best person to secure childcare may be the district lead or the team leaders. In my district, for the first five years that we had FET teams, team leaders at each school identified their childcare providers. In the first year of the COVID-19 pandemic, we shifted to virtual FET meetings, and childcare was not needed (although we did often have pizzas delivered to participating families so that they didn't need to worry about cooking a meal before or after the team meeting). When we returned to in-person FET meetings during the second year of the pandemic and securing providers became very challenging, we were lucky to forge a partnership with a local high school that helped provide volunteers. Heading into the third year of the pandemic, as that partnership dissolved and our number of FET teams grew, I realized as the district lead that it would greatly support team leaders if I held the responsibility of securing childcare support for all teams.

While it was initially quite challenging to find support for all schools that needed childcare, ultimately a three-pronged approach worked well for us: paying trained providers from a local organization that had the capacity to support half our schools; partnering with a nonprofit that was centered on male high school students pairing up with their mothers to volunteer and complete needed service hours; and our high schools asking student leaders to earn volunteer hours or receive gift cards by offering their help for their school's FET meetings.

Meals

Food is a key element for a connective and successful gathering, so it's good to prioritize determining the provider of the meal for your first FET gathering. Think about what kind of food would be satisfying for most team members and easy to procure since team leaders juggle a lot of preparation in advance of the first meeting. Team leaders can discuss some of the best local options and should try to select a meal that is likely to be enjoyed by participants, easy to order, and either picked up or delivered. Dinner can be purchased from a nearby restaurant, it can be bought at a market and reheated, or you can hire a parent in your school community to prepare the meal. If you take the latter route, confer with your front office team beforehand to discuss how this community member will be paid for their efforts. When buying dinner from a restaurant, decide whether it will be delivered or picked up by you or a colleague. Think about a colleague or two who might be able to help set up the food, drinks, plates, cups, napkins, and utensils so that ideally you can focus your time right before the first meeting on conferring with your other team leaders and district lead and taking care of other final logistics.

Organization

Figure 3.1 is a checklist team leaders can use to keep track of the tasks they need to complete during the first few weeks of the school year.

There are a host of important tasks for the district lead to accomplish in the opening weeks of school as well. Figure 3.2 is a checklist of the timeliest ones to tackle in the opening month of the school year and before teams hold their first meetings.

Tasks for Team Leaders During the First Few Weeks of the School Year

☐ Choose meeting dates, times, and locations.

☐ Check your school and district's master calendar to avoid overlap with other events that might impact team members' attendance.

☐ Send monthly calendar invites for all FET team meetings through the end of the school year to the entire staff and the district lead at least two weeks prior to your first team meeting.

☐ Schedule monthly hour-long planning sessions with your other team leaders and your district lead.

☐ Add your school's FET meeting day and time, and your planning day and time, to a districtwide FET calendar document.

☐ Hold your first meeting planning session with your fellow team leaders and your district lead (in the second or third week of the school year).

☐ Have the district lead send calendar invites to team leaders for every monthly planning session for the rest of the school year.

☐ Decide, with fellow team leaders, how you will distribute responsibilities among yourselves and other team members.

☐ Schedule interpretation support for at least the first meeting, if you already know what languages team members will need interpreted.

☐ Schedule a childcare provider for at least the first meeting.

☐ Determine the source of your meal for the first meeting.

☐ Identify the account code that will be used for all FET team budget expenses and identify the front office colleague to go to for all questions related to purchases.

Figure 3.1: Key logistics checklist for team leaders.

*Visit **go.SolutionTree.com/diversityandequity** for a free reproducible version of this figure.*

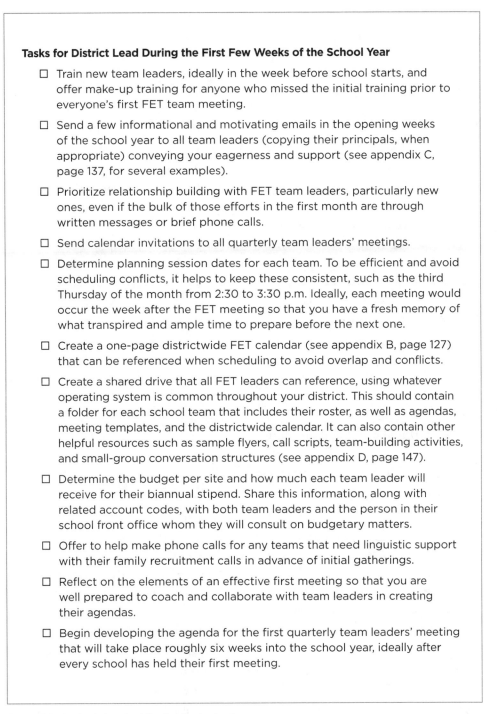

Tasks for District Lead During the First Few Weeks of the School Year

☐ Train new team leaders, ideally in the week before school starts, and offer make-up training for anyone who missed the initial training prior to everyone's first FET team meeting.

☐ Send a few informational and motivating emails in the opening weeks of the school year to all team leaders (copying their principals, when appropriate) conveying your eagerness and support (see appendix C, page 137, for several examples).

☐ Prioritize relationship building with FET team leaders, particularly new ones, even if the bulk of those efforts in the first month are through written messages or brief phone calls.

☐ Send calendar invitations to all quarterly team leaders' meetings.

☐ Determine planning session dates for each team. To be efficient and avoid scheduling conflicts, it helps to keep these consistent, such as the third Thursday of the month from 2:30 to 3:30 p.m. Ideally, each meeting would occur the week after the FET meeting so that you have a fresh memory of what transpired and ample time to prepare before the next one.

☐ Create a one-page districtwide FET calendar (see appendix B, page 127) that can be referenced when scheduling to avoid overlap and conflicts.

☐ Create a shared drive that all FET leaders can reference, using whatever operating system is common throughout your district. This should contain a folder for each school team that includes their roster, as well as agendas, meeting templates, and the districtwide calendar. It can also contain other helpful resources such as sample flyers, call scripts, team-building activities, and small-group conversation structures (see appendix D, page 147).

☐ Determine the budget per site and how much each team leader will receive for their biannual stipend. Share this information, along with related account codes, with both team leaders and the person in their school front office whom they will consult on budgetary matters.

☐ Offer to help make phone calls for any teams that need linguistic support with their family recruitment calls in advance of initial gatherings.

☐ Reflect on the elements of an effective first meeting so that you are well prepared to coach and collaborate with team leaders in creating their agendas.

☐ Begin developing the agenda for the first quarterly team leaders' meeting that will take place roughly six weeks into the school year, ideally after every school has held their first meeting.

Figure 3.2: Key logistics checklist for district lead.

*Visit **go.SolutionTree.com/diversityandequity** for a free reproducible version of this figure.*

Recruit Team Members

Now that you have established most of the groundwork for setting up a FET team, it is time to focus on perhaps the most important task: recruitment. We explored in chapter 2 (page 31) who is part of the team and why they are instrumental to the team's functioning and success. Now we will turn to the how—effective steps to identify and inspire stakeholders to join the team.

While it is always possible to incorporate new team members well into the school year, it pays off to front-load outreach efforts to have a strong turnout from both families and staff members. The first few FET gatherings often inspire participants around the purpose and are both connective and uplifting. As a result, stakeholders who attend these initial meetings usually become consistent members of the team. That said, the steady elements present in any FET meeting support new families or staff in feeling welcomed, so do not feel too much pressure to inspire a massive turnout at your first meeting. Since FET will likely be both a new acronym and unfamiliar concept for staff and families alike, remember the aim is to start small, as a team of at least five educators and five family members.

Since FET team leaders hold so many other responsibilities in their professional and personal lives, the most efficient and effective way to scaffold recruitment in the first four to six weeks of the school year (in advance of the first FET meeting) is to focus first on staff and then on families. The appendices provide numerous resources for outreach, including an "Overview of FET to Share With Stakeholders" reproducible (page 145) that you may find useful in these efforts.

Connect With Colleagues

It is a universal truth that educators are hampered by overwhelm and usually juggle more responsibilities than one person should hold. After their full days at school, it is no small request to ask for their presence at an evening event, whether that entails staying late or returning to school after a brief stint at home. However, as we explored in chapter 1 (page 19), in the wake of the pandemic, educators are both more aware of the importance of partnering with families and often personally and professionally interested in feeling a greater sense of community with other adults.

In FET, it's slightly easier to reach the aim of at least five educators because one or two of the team leaders are typically staff members, and if the principal or other school leader attends as well, that often means simply needing to recruit two additional staff members. Since this involves staff voluntarily giving up an evening at home, one-on-one outreach is usually the most effective.

If the school has set up FET as a committee that staff signed up for, a core team has already been established. However, you still want to extend an invite to other staff, particularly those who work closely with many of the families that will attend FET (for example, an English language development teacher, family liaison, or school counselor) or who have demonstrated a particular passion or strength in connecting with families.

In addition to the team leaders and principal personally inviting specific colleagues, this is the time to lay the foundation for ongoing staff outreach strategies. These can include sending an email to the whole staff using enticing talking points about FET, securing two minutes at a staff meeting before the first FET gathering to invite others to attend, or sending a calendar invitation to the entire staff for every team meeting for the remainder of the school year.

For new teams, it is also wise to revisit the list of staff who attended the informational meeting the previous spring to recall who has already expressed interest in FET. For existing teams, it can be effective to have family members who have been actively involved on the team to personally invite a staff member or two.

Finally, it is important to emphasize that the great majority of staff members choose to return after attending FET once, so the invite should spark their interest and underscore that by coming to the first FET meeting they are not committing to regularly attending. The delicious free dinner and time to connect more personally with underrepresented families are also two strong selling points.

The following are some more tips for recruiting colleagues.

- In the spring before the fall launch of the FET team and in the first few weeks of school, engage in one-on-one conversations with colleagues you think might be interested in participating.

- Ask your principal if they can designate FET as a committee this year, which would guarantee a certain number of participating staff are steady team members.

- Ask colleagues to sign up to visit a FET meeting during a designated month or invite grade-level or department teams to attend a specific monthly gathering so that families can meet a larger portion of the staff throughout a given school year.

- Ask your principal for a few minutes at a staff meeting to share about FET and see who is interested in attending the first team meeting.

- Draw upon the FET purpose statements in chapter 1 (page 23) to help guide you during informal conversations with colleagues.

- Be persistent via informal conversations, emails, and so on until you have identified at least three colleagues who will join you, your team leaders, and your school leader at the first meeting.

- If you are having a challenging time identifying staff to participate, consider starting with colleagues who are newer to the school, as they are often more receptive to taking on new responsibilities, or conversely staff who are settled in enough that they have the bandwidth to try out a new opportunity.

Connect With Families

It is beneficial to make a full list of all the families that you want to invite to FET. If possible, come up with this list and plant the seed with prospective families the previous spring. As you reflect on who to invite, keep in mind the guidance of Karen Mapp and her colleagues (2017) about all equitable partnership efforts: "design a plan for outreach that reflects an understanding of the diverse families present in the school" (pp. 30–31).

Regardless of whether you contacted families in the spring, it is important to begin letting families know about the purpose of FET and the date of the first meeting at least two weeks before it takes place and immediately after the first planning meeting transpires. If possible, record a two- to three-minute digital commercial for FET that primarily gives an overview of the five Ws that will entice families to attend: what a FET team is, why attending it will be enjoyable and meaningful, who it focuses on, and when and where the first meeting will take place. From there, teams tend to find the greatest success through one-on-one personalized outreach to parents and other family members.

Phone calls are an excellent, personalized way to outreach. While families ideally hear about FET from multiple sources, the most likely staff members to make calls are the team leaders, principal, community liaison, assistant principal, and teachers who work with the largest number of students from underrepresented families. Due to privacy policies, if the team has a parent leader or two, they typically can make calls after the first meeting, once families have granted permission for their contact information to be shared with the parent leaders.

The following are some more tips for recruiting families.

- Clarify which families you want to include in the FET team (for example, all Spanish speakers, families that speak a language other than English at home, parents who were born in countries outside of the United States, parents of color, and so on) and create a potential roster with names, phone numbers, and other pertinent information.

- In the three to four weeks prior to the first meeting, work with your school administrative team to ask each staff member to recommend at least one family for FET.

- Recruiting families to join gatherings is a continuous process. The following are effective pathways and options for inviting families to both the first and subsequent meetings.

  ‣ Set up a FET table for back-to-school night. Provide copies of an information sheet, in multiple languages if relevant, that parents can take with them to reference later (see an example in appendix C, page 137).

  ‣ Invite family members when you see them in person before, during, or after school.

  ‣ Share information directly with newcomer families or colleagues who work closely with multilingual students.

  ‣ Send students home with a flyer invitation to the first meeting, or share these flyers with colleagues who make home visits. Some schools have given stickers to students or an invitation that resembles a wristwatch that students can wear home and includes a QR code that links to more information.

  ‣ Send an email to all prospective FET families (see an example in appendix C, page 137), or send a text via a two-communication app that translates the message into the family's preferred language. Consider asking your principal to complete this outreach effort, knowing the impact it has for families to hear directly from the principal.

‣ Create a short video invitation to share with families.

‣ Include a short blurb about FET in your school's parent newsletter.

‣ Create a visually appealing FET poster and place it in a highly visible area of your school.

‣ Call each prospective family member individually to invite them to the first meeting (and draw upon your community liaison or other colleagues for support with these calls if needed). Additionally, you can ask your school administrative support to help you record an auto dialer voice message to send to a larger group of families (see an example in appendix C, page 137).

It pays off to be detail oriented, methodical, and well organized in your efforts to both build a foundation for the initial team meeting and recruit team members.

Conclusion

FET teams thrive when their leaders are well trained and address crucial logistics in both a proactive and scaffolded fashion. Team leaders also build a strong foundation when they partner with principals to strategically recruit both families and colleagues to join the first FET meeting.

In the next chapter, we will walk through every facet of planning and executing the first meeting. Our goal is to ensure that the first FET gathering is dynamic and effective. Doing so in a thorough fashion will enhance future gatherings throughout the year.

Questions for Reflection and Discussion

1. What elements of FET do you think are most essential to highlight when training new FET leaders?

2. In terms of all the vital logistics covered in this chapter, where do you anticipate the greatest challenges or the most likely pitfalls in launching your teams? How can you proactively navigate them?

3. What existing resources can you immediately harness to support some of the most crucial logistics, such as interpretation, childcare, and so on?

4. What existing human or financial resources can you leverage in your school or district to begin launching this work?

5. What combination of strategies will you implement to maximize the likelihood of strong turnout by family members at the first FET meeting? Which colleagues would be the best ones to help you in this effort?

CHAPTER 4

Making Your First FET Meeting a Success

There is a Mexican saying,
Hablando se entiende la gente.
Talking to one another
We understand one another.
I would add: And listening
We understand even better.

—Sandra Cisneros

Once you have set a solid foundation for your FET team, it is time to plan the first meeting and get clear on every detail. Since the team is a new concept and structure for most or all stakeholders, it is important to do everything possible to make the initial gathering connective, enjoyable, meaningful, and uplifting. In doing so, everyone will want to return for future meetings and feel motivated to invite new people to join as well.

A significant part of what makes FET gatherings distinct from other school meetings that involve families is the amount of thought and time that goes into crafting the agenda for each team meeting. What makes FET a unique space for families and educators alike is the confluence of these elements and what unfolds in the ninety minutes between them walking through the doors and heading home. In this chapter, we will take an in-depth look at how to ensure a meeting will be engaging and successful, how to create the meeting agenda, and the components and sequence of a typical FET meeting.

How to Plan a Compelling FET Team Meeting

FET is a vehicle for fostering unusually strong family-educator partnerships. Having a consistent structure for meetings and developing a clear agenda are vital for FET teams to flourish. Although part of the spirit of FET is responding to what parents share and not being overly bound to the agenda, a consistent and proven structure makes all the difference. While each FET team shapes the contents of meetings based on their unique school community, there are certain core elements that are consistent across all teams.

Preparation

As discussed in chapter 3 (page 43), the success of any FET meeting is grounded in thoughtful planning. Team leaders typically spend an hour, usually with the district lead, designing each agenda, with an emphasis on fostering connection from the opening minutes, centering parent voices, focusing on tangible change efforts, and closing with a sense of unity. Whereas in a typical planning session for a FET meeting we tend to spend roughly ten minutes reflecting on the last meeting, another ten minutes discussing the logistics, and forty minutes creating the actual agenda, for the first gathering we use about thirty minutes to flesh out logistics and the final thirty minutes to craft the agenda.

Some of the top facilitators in the world, such as Priya Parker (2018), have affirmed that when gatherings "crackle and flourish," it is in large part due to how much time, creativity, and intentionality leaders wove into the planning (p. xiv). Often, it is the small decisions that make a gathering soar. In her experiences facilitating meetings everywhere from the White House to the board room, Parker (2018) found that "90 percent of what makes a gathering successful is put in place beforehand" (p. 149).

Effective delegation is critical to preparation. As organizational performance experts Jeffrey Pfeffer and Robert Sutton (2006) write, "It is hard to build a system where others can succeed if the leader believes he or she needs to make every important decision, and knows better than anyone else what to do and how to do it" (p. 211). Savvy FET leaders consistently find ways to both lighten their load and harness the wisdom and support of others in the planning phase, the actual meeting, and the follow-up communication and outreach. Figure 4.1 provides a list of roles that facilitators can delegate.

Roles to Delegate

Premeeting greeter _____

Person to pick up meal _____

Notetaker _____

Participant tracker _____

Timekeeper _____

Small-group reporters _____

Spokesperson to share out with staff _____

Spokesperson to share out with families _____

Figure 4.1: Roles for FET team leaders to delegate.

*Visit **go.SolutionTree.com/diversityandequity** for a free reproducible version of this figure.*

Another component to address before shifting to the actual agenda is creating a short list of the materials that will be needed during the meeting. Besides the supplies needed for dinner and resources that will help the childcare provider, this list usually includes items such as name tags, sign-in sheet, pens, markers, sticky notes, chart paper, and so on.

Figure 4.2 is a premeeting checklist that will help team leaders lay the foundation for an effective gathering before anyone has arrived. FET meetings start smoothly if team leaders address the following elements; conversely, meetings begin in a frantic fashion if these elements are neglected or completed last minute.

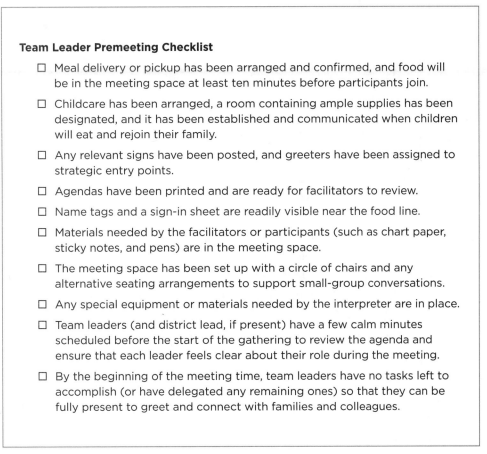

Team Leader Premeeting Checklist

☐ Meal delivery or pickup has been arranged and confirmed, and food will be in the meeting space at least ten minutes before participants join.

☐ Childcare has been arranged, a room containing ample supplies has been designated, and it has been established and communicated when children will eat and rejoin their family.

☐ Any relevant signs have been posted, and greeters have been assigned to strategic entry points.

☐ Agendas have been printed and are ready for facilitators to review.

☐ Name tags and a sign-in sheet are readily visible near the food line.

☐ Materials needed by the facilitators or participants (such as chart paper, sticky notes, and pens) are in the meeting space.

☐ The meeting space has been set up with a circle of chairs and any alternative seating arrangements to support small-group conversations.

☐ Any special equipment or materials needed by the interpreter are in place.

☐ Team leaders (and district lead, if present) have a few calm minutes scheduled before the start of the gathering to review the agenda and ensure that each leader feels clear about their role during the meeting.

☐ By the beginning of the meeting time, team leaders have no tasks left to accomplish (or have delegated any remaining ones) so that they can be fully present to greet and connect with families and colleagues.

Figure 4.2: FET premeeting checklist for team leaders.

*Visit **go.SolutionTree.com/diversityandequity** for a free reproducible version of this figure.*

Agenda

One of the key elements that distinguishes FET from most other school-based meetings is the degree to which team leaders and the district lead are purposeful and thorough in determining the sequence and structure of the agenda. While most educators know that strong engagement for their own students often grows from detailed planning efforts, they usually have little experience attending engaging meetings and even less experience designing and leading such meetings.

Over the course of my fifteen years co-leading SEL and cultural responsiveness workshops for educators outside of my school district, participants have regularly commented that it was one of the best professional development experiences of their career. I noticed that they were more consistently engaged throughout these twenty-hour weekend retreats than most of my colleagues were in one-hour trainings at our schools.

When I reflected on what led to such high levels of engagement in these workshops, I realized one significant factor was our rigorous planning efforts and attention to detail. The ten hours or so my colleagues and I devoted to planning were as vital to the success of these gatherings as the actual content.

Unfortunately, due to the inordinate pressures on their time, most team leaders' first instinct is to plan their FET meeting as quickly as possible. However, in my first years as the district lead for FET, I noticed that when we rushed and tried to determine both the logistics and agenda in thirty or forty minutes, we either had an inadequate plan or paid the price during the actual FET gathering. Therefore, in my fifth year as district lead I made it a built-in expectation that we would spend an hour together planning each ninety-minute FET meeting. This coincided with the year when (after several years of trial and error) we finally landed on an optimal agenda structure.

While it can sometimes feel like considerable labor for a single, ninety-minute meeting, the effort put into the planning process pays off because a great first gathering usually translates into participants feeling eager to return and trusting team leaders to effectively steer the ship.

As seasoned facilitators know well, no meeting goes exactly as planned. Part of the art of excellent facilitation is to be responsive in the moment to the inevitable curveballs. Or as one FET team leader put it at the end of her first year of leadership, "Plan down to the minute and then know that some people will show up five to fifteen minutes late and all of that will go out the window."

Figure 4.3 shows an agenda that was created for the first meeting of a new FET team.

September FET Meeting

Date, Time, and Location: September 8, 2022, 6:00–7:30 p.m., Angevine Library
Meal: Karen will pick up
Childcare: Local group contracted
Interpreter: Tonya
Staff Communication Outreach: Karen and Will
- Informal outreach to Emiliano, Laura, Micaela, Sarah, Susan, and Julie

Family Communication Outreach:
- School voicemail to all Spanish-speaking families with script (Will)
- Flyer for back-to-school night (Micaela)
- Email to families (Karen)
- Reminder flyer (Sonia)

Notetaker: Ari
Timekeeper: Julie

Materials: Karen; materials include sign-in sheet, name tags, blank chart paper, sticky notes, pens, chart with image of tree, and tape

Agenda

6:00–6:15: Meal and Informal Connection

6:15–6:20: Team-Builder 3-2-1 activity (Ari)

6:20–6:30: Opening Circle (Will and Ari)

- Ask family members to tell the team their name and their student's name and grade.
- Ask staff to tell the team their name, the subject they teach, and how many years they have been at our school.
- Ask all to also mention a summer activity they enjoy doing with their family.

6:30–6:35: Quick Update and Overview of Tonight's Agenda (Ari and Sarah)

- What is the purpose of FET, and what are the principal's hopes for the team? (Ari and Sarah)
- Where are we going tonight? (Karen, followed by transition statement)

6:35–6:45: Shared Values Activity [first or second meeting only] (Ari)

- Ask team members to discuss the following questions in a small group.
  - What are two or three values that are really important to your family? Talk about them.
  - Which one is most important? Write it on sticky note and post it on the roots section of the chart paper with the image of a tree.
- Read aloud the values written on the sticky notes and tell the team that these values will be the foundation for the team's efforts this school year. The fruit on the branches will be the projects that emerge from the team's shared values. They will add the fruits of their collective efforts to this poster at the final gathering of the year.

6:45–7:15: Meaningful Dialogue in Small Groups With Recorder and Chart Paper (Ari)

- Ask team members to discuss the following questions in a small group.
  - How are the first few weeks of school going for you and for your student?
  - What has been challenging this year or last spring? Where do you continue to see barriers between Latino families and the staff?

7:15–7:20: Summary of Final Logistics and Next Steps

- Our next meeting is Tuesday, October 4, at 6:00 p.m. Dinner and childcare will be provided.
- What would you like for dinner next month?
- Please spread the word and ask your friends to join us.

7:20–7:30: Closing Circle (Will)

- Ask participants to tell, in one word, how they are feeling.
- Let them know it is OK to pass or repeat what someone else said.
- Thank participants for attending.

Source: © 2023 by Angevine Middle School. Used with permission.

Figure: 4.3: Sample new FET team meeting agenda.

*Visit **go.SolutionTree.com/diversityandequity** for a free blank reproducible version of this figure.*

Every so often there is a FET team leader who goes rogue and is not receptive to support from others. I share here the experience of one team, as it sheds light on several key elements that drive FET's success.

A new FET leader, Roxane, was not interested in receiving district support. In Roxane's third year, a new teacher, Tracy, became one of her co-leaders. Tracy was eager to benefit from the FET structures and strategies that were serving other schools. In the first weeks of the school year, I reached out to every FET team to offer my coaching support and set up planning sessions. Tracy told me that she was finding it difficult to find time to plan with Roxane and the other leader. Her impression was that her fellow team leads wanted to have more unstructured meetings that were focused on hanging out, listening to music, and chatting over a meal.

The day of the monthly FET meeting, upon her principal's request, Tracy shared their agenda, which was roughly three lines long. I reshared the meeting agenda template that other schools use with Tracy, and she created a more robust agenda that better resembled what other teams' plans look like, which she used for the FET meeting that afternoon.

As always, I was rooting for them to have a deeply engaging and meaning-ful gathering. Despite some conversation about potential team goals and each parent having the chance to speak at least once, the meeting was not a success. There were many choices the team leaders made or did not make that contrib-uted to a meeting that was riddled with many awkward moments of silence.

Here are some of the biggest takeaways from this first meeting in terms of why it did not crackle with the connective and engaging feel of effective initial gatherings.

- The team leaders took months, not weeks, to find time for their first planning session.
- When they gathered for the planning session, they did not form a con-crete agenda.
- Instead of having everyone sit in a circle, participants sat in front of small tables around the room. Two team leaders sat at the front of the room, and Roxane stood for most of the meeting. Unlike other schools where the group quickly feels like one unified team, this group felt fragmented.
- They did not have a team-building activity. After the meal concluded and everyone briefly introduced themselves, it was evident as the first questions were posed that some participants did not feel comfortable enough to voice their thoughts to the whole group.
- The agenda included several great discussion questions. Unfortunately, team members were not told whether they should discuss the questions with a partner or in small groups. Due to the confusion, a few seconds after the question was shared, someone spoke to the whole group, and the time for people to generate ideas and build confidence in their voices evaporated.

As the meeting approached its end time and the only component remaining was the closing activity, I witnessed something that I have never seen in hundreds of FET gatherings. A few parents, prompted by a glance at the clock on the wall or their diminishing interest, stood up and began to leave the room. The team leaders did not encourage them to wait a few minutes before leaving, and the meeting ended abruptly, without an uplifting and unifying closing activity.

While several interesting ideas and potential goals for the team emerged throughout the conversation and the team leaders all had good intentions, the difference between this first meeting and the typical initial gathering was stark. A great first meeting helps teams quickly gain momentum.

Essential Elements of a FET Team Meeting

Most FET gatherings consistently have the same eight elements:

1. Meal and informal connection
2. Team-builder
3. Opening circle
4. Quick updates and meeting overview
5. Family learning time
6. Meaningful dialogue
7. Final logistics and next steps
8. Purposeful closure

Through several years of trial and error, we landed on this optimal structure that is intentional about fostering engagement, centering parent voices, sparking mutual learning, identifying action steps, and consistently building trust and a sense of team unity.

The following sections describe each of the necessary elements of a FET meeting and how much time during the actual FET meeting to dedicate to it.

Meal and Informal Connection (fifteen minutes)

As we all have likely experienced in our connection with our own families, communities, and colleagues, breaking bread together helps us build or deepen bonds. A shared meal is a key ingredient to a successful gathering (Woolley & Fishbach, 2017). It's essential to help families to feel more comfortable, and to help staff have the energy to participate after a full day working with students.

In the earliest years of FET, a few team leaders—mostly due to wanting to save the time involved in procuring food and setting it up, or thinking that it would be a distraction—opted to not include a meal in their meetings. Not surprisingly, I noticed that it was more difficult for families and staff on these particular teams to relax and engage in the first half of the meeting. It also became clear in the early years of FET that the one team that consistently achieved the strongest sense of community happened to be the same one that always built in time for dinner. In addition, their meals were often made by families at their school or on their team, and consistently reflected the culinary preferences of most team members.

While I initially did not want to require all team leaders to provide a meal at their gathering, it felt like we were not being culturally responsive or considerate when we left dinner out of the equation. Providing a meal is a caring and practical gesture that shows that the school values both families and educators giving their personal time in the evening. It also fosters a sense of comfort that allows participants to relax and more easily engage with others.

Based on these factors, as I revamped the common meeting agenda template in my fifth year as FET district lead, I made it a universal practice that teams eat a meal and engage in unstructured conversations the first fifteen minutes of every FET meeting. Some participants may still be eating after that time and can briefly set aside their plate for the team-building exercise, and then resume enjoying their meal as we move on to other parts of the agenda.

Team-Builder (three to five minutes)

Before the opening circle, the team members stand and engage in a team-builder, a brief game that reliably energizes and connects. This can be either a whole-group or paired activity. The undeniable benefits of team-builders are that they often spark laughter and connection, foster greater emotional safety, and lead each participant to feel more energized and present. At the first and second meetings, there can be value in doing more than one team-builder to help accelerate building trust and rapport. For a list of team-building activities you can use in your meetings, see appendix D (page 147).

For FET to succeed, it is vital that team leaders create a space in which families candidly reveal the barriers that schools have unintentionally erected, as well as share any blind spots and biases they see in educators. Equally important, educators need to feel safe enough to admit uncertainty or areas of challenge, and not become defensive when parents make constructive suggestions. Team-builders are a great way to facilitate this safe environment. They not only foster joy and a sense of unity but also energize adult brains (particularly important considering that FET meetings begin in the evening) and help everyone contribute insightfully. In his research, author Shawn Achor (2018) finds that the brain is 31 percent more efficient when it experiences a positive state or emotion compared to a neutral mood.

According to research on building an effective team, the key ingredient is creating a strong sense of psychological safety for all members (Edmondson, 2019). When we feel safe, we perform better, take more risks, and are more willing to be vulnerable (Duhigg, 2016).

Fostering strong levels of psychological safety is particularly critical for underrepresented families because of the discrimination and bias they may have encountered in their own schooling. However, we are not creating the risk-free environment of a "safe space," but instead cultivating a "brave space" that "acknowledges the unavoidable risk, struggle, and discomfort that accompany authentic engagement" (Krownapple, 2017, p. 48). In short, we want to gradually build higher levels of psychological safety to support each participant's capacity to be vulnerable, share honestly, and effectively dialogue across difference (Auerbach, 2012). How is psychological safety fostered from the opening minutes? We do everything possible to help participants relax and put down their guards so they can connect authentically.

At one high school's inaugural meeting, these activities played a critical role in helping everyone show up in a more relaxed, authentic fashion. At this meeting, the four teachers sat in a line of desks, and as the parents filed in, they occupied the row of desks across from the teachers. Once it happened, it was too late to shift the setup, which felt more like an encounter between two debate squads than the opening meeting of a team that would address decades of disconnect between the school and Latino families. We played Gotcha, one of my favorite SEL team-builders (see appendix D, page 147, for this and other team-building activities). In less than five minutes, we went from awkward silence and zero conversation to laughter from every participant. Laughter creates a sense of sameness and coherence, and is a key element needed to create trustful spaces that are safe for authentic sharing and soulful connection (Palmer, 2004).

After the team-builder, the transition to the ritual of an opening circle is smoother. Across a host of diverse cultures, people have been gathering in circles, which flatten hierarchies and accelerate equalizing participants, for centuries (Fisher & Frey, 2022).

Opening Circle (five to ten minutes)

The opening minutes set the tone for the entire gathering. The importance of this crucial yet brief portion of a meeting is often overlooked. As Parker (2018) writes:

> In the first few moments of a gathering, we are all . . . reading cues and asking ourselves: What do I think of this gathering? Am I in good hands? Is the host nervous? Should I be? What's going to happen here? Is this worth my time? Do I belong? Do I want to belong? The opening is, therefore, an important opportunity to establish the legitimacy of your gathering. (p. 173)

In this part of the meeting, ask parents to share their name and their child's name and grade level, followed by a response to a prompt that changes each meeting. The staff members on the team also conclude their introductions by answering the prompt, but they share their name and their role at the school (and sometimes the names of their own children and what schools they attend).

The overarching purpose of the opening circle is to support every team member in feeling seen and valued as part of the group. It also provides a vital opportunity for each participant to bring their voice briefly into the room so that they are more comfortable doing so in greater depth later in the meeting. The prompt is usually something that does not require team members to reveal too much personal info but enough to build a sense of the commonalities and differences that help us get to know the human beyond the role, be it parent or educator. For example, in September you might ask everyone to share one of their favorite parts of fall ("the way that the leaves change colors"), or in November you might ask them to share something that they feel particularly grateful for ("extra time with family over the holidays").

Knowing how much most people long for community and appreciate being heard, it is easy for these circles to last longer than five to ten minutes, so it's important to pose a prompt that can be answered in a word, phrase, or couple of sentences. To increase the likelihood that all team members heed these instructions, we typically have team leaders share first to model the brevity and then proceed around the circle.

Quick Updates and Meeting Overview (two to five minutes)

The updates and overview agenda item provides a brief opportunity to accomplish a few things.

- Share any announcements that are pertinent about the team's progress or any school-wide events or information that would be beneficial for family members to know.

- Provide a brief overview of the purpose of FET in a way that will optimally resonate with each participant. You might also include here (or in the opening circle) time for some or all team members to share what drew them to join this initial meeting or what their hopes are for the team this school year.

- Offer a succinct overview of the main activities or topics the team will explore that evening.

Particularly at the first meeting, when most team members have such a surface-level understanding of FET or no idea what a meeting is like, this brief preview helps people feel less anxious and more enthusiastic.

Family Learning Time (fifteen to twenty minutes)

After the mealtime connections, team-builder, and opening circle—and before moving into the central conversation—teams can invite guest speakers that parents requested. The guest speakers can share meaningful information, spark dialogue, and in the spirit of mutuality that FET is founded on, often gain insight from what family members share. For instance, at one team meeting in my district, parents had requested that district nurses share the latest news on COVID-19 protocols. Both staff and families asked them questions and learned from what they shared, and the nurses learned more about what information families would most need moving forward.

Other topics that teams might explore in family learning time include mental health resources, digital literacy, postgraduate opportunities, substance use prevention, and the role of the school counselor. It's best to engage families at the second or third FET meeting of the year in a brainstorming session around topics or speakers that they would enjoy for future gatherings.

While sharing information with families that helps them better understand the workings of the school becomes an important part of most FET meetings, it is uncommon to include this aspect of the agenda in the first meeting of the year. However, sometimes certain topics are so timely and important that a team might integrate this into their first meeting to front-load this key learning.

Meaningful Dialogue (twenty-five to thirty minutes)

Half an hour into the ninety-minute gathering, it's time to dive into the heart of the meeting. Meaningful dialogue time is focused on conversations that center parent voices and elicit staff perspectives as well. Over time, ongoing dialogue in cross-cultural settings leads to better communication, stronger relationships, and deeper levels of trust (Campbell Jones, Keeny, & Campbell Jones, 2020)

Team leaders might begin the conversation by posing a thought-provoking question, such as:

- How has the year gone so far for you and your child?
- How do you feel about the level of communication from your child's teachers or the school as a whole? What has been helpful, and what could be improved?
- What challenges or barriers have you seen or experienced regarding the school?
- How might we make learning more interesting so that your children are more eager to come to school?
- What are you most interested in discussing or learning about this year?

Alternatively, you might go straight into open forum time where parents can bring up timely issues that are important to them (for example, concerns about the paucity of communication from teachers). As one of our FET leaders put it, by creating space for "our parents to bring to the table their issues, concerns, and so on, they have provided us with opportunities to build resources that best serve them, and to bring resources to our staff and school to better serve our students."

Sometimes you may ask questions and then shift to open forum consecutively. Regardless of the path, the approach mirrors what Ann Ishimaru (2020) describes as the four principles to more just schools.

1. Begin with family priorities, interests, concerns, and knowledge.
2. Transform power.
3. Build reciprocity and agency.
4. Undertake changes as collective inquiry.

Posing great questions—either identified in advance or generated thoughtfully in the moment—is essential for creating engaging FET gatherings, strengthening cross-cultural relationships, and sparking transformative and equitable change (Campbell Jones et al., 2020). See appendix D (page 147) for a list of potential questions to use in FET gatherings.

As thought-provoking and meaningful questions lead teams to engage in collective inquiry, they make it clear that we are all learners, which is especially important for our educators to be reminded of. Educators do not need to be experts in this space, and their humility and growth mindset enables family members to also show up more fully. As such, I cannot overstate the critical importance of educators doing most of the listening in order to forge truly authentic and shared partnerships and build community (Mapp et al., 2022).

From back-to-school nights to parent-teacher conferences, educators tend to do a disproportionate amount of the talking. I was guilty of this as a teacher and principal, feeling that this was how I demonstrated my competency and maintained control of the conversation. In cases where a FET team has struggled, it has often been because educators dominate the discussion time. Conversely, in spaces where power differences have been effectively flattened, authentic speaking and deep listening lead to many benefits. As Margaret Wheatley (2009) puts it, "Listening and talking to one another heals our divisions and makes us brave again" (p. 15).

How do we make it clear from the very first meeting that we actually want both parents and educators to challenge the status quo and see FET as a vehicle for transformation? We must be very intentional in the first meeting to ensure that parents have ample time to talk. It's one thing to say that we are going to prioritize hearing families' perspectives and another thing to actually do it.

To catalyze participation, ask team members to talk with a partner or small group before sharing with the whole team. This strategy works particularly well with newer teams or when parents or staff do not feel comfortable to confidently bring forth their voices. As you guide the team into generating action projects, you can also break into small working groups for fifteen to thirty minutes, then have everyone report their progress and solicit additional input or conversation when they return to the larger group. Trust and collaboration in FET are built one meeting at a time. Each gathering is a building block toward developing a strong foundation for candid conversations and co-created change efforts.

In terms of the flow of this core part of the meeting, we typically spend fifteen to twenty minutes in small groups, give each group a few minutes to report back highlights of their conversations, and then finish with a brief whole-group chat that is sparked by a question, such as "What did you find most interesting in what you just heard?"

Most first FET meetings leave everyone feeling satisfied from the engaging conversations and hungry to dive more deeply into all the topics that surfaced. As facilitators, we capture many of participants' ideas on chart paper to visually demonstrate how much we value everyone's contributions and also to give us a detailed record that we can refer to as we plan for the second FET gathering.

Final Logistics and Next Steps (two to five minutes)

During this short portion of the meeting between the dialogue and closing circle, remind team members of the date of the next meeting. At this first gathering, we take the opportunity to honor families' preferences and give them decision-making power by asking them if this day and time worked well for them or if they would prefer another option.

You may also ask them what type of meal they'd like for dinner at the second gathering, or what specific restaurant they might like. While this is a small gesture, it conveys again to families that this is a different kind of school meeting than they are used to in that they have voice in shaping it. It communicates that the school isn't deciding everything for them, which is typically how the details for even the most family-centered events such as back-to-school night are determined (Mapp et al., 2017).

Finally, take a few moments to summarize the major topics or ideas that surfaced and speak in general terms about next steps. I'll never forget one of the best pieces of feedback I received as a principal after one of our staff leadership team meetings came to a close, when a teacher told me, "We have these great conversations but we don't leave the time to synthesize what we've discussed and get clear on next steps and who is responsible for them."

While not every FET meeting leads to this type of clarity, it helps the team build momentum and maintain focus (and earns the trust of participants who want to see follow-through on concrete action steps) when we state succinctly what we heard and commit to any next steps. In the aim to build a festive environment, some teams have held a raffle to gift prizes to a few randomly selected family members in attendance.

Purposeful Closure (five minutes)

Participants disproportionately remember the first and last 5 percent of a gathering, yet we often treat these as afterthoughts (Parker, 2018). We also know that both families and educators are more likely to consistently return to future FET meetings if they feel energized, seen, and an integral part of a team. For these reasons, pause the conversation and consistently designate five minutes for the closing.

However, most schools do not heed this wisdom in most meetings they hold, as there is either no plan for meaningful closure or other parts of the gathering run over their time allotment. When this occurs, there isn't time left to revisit the purpose, foster a sense of unity among participants, or take a few minutes to engage in an uplifting final activity. As one of our FET leaders reflected at the end of her first year guiding her team, "Finish with connection, fun, and parent voice, not logistics and announcements."

When the closing activity is carefully and strategically selected, the end of a gathering can help sustain participants' positive feelings or elevate them. Too many gatherings in school settings end abruptly with "Sorry, our time is up," or close with logistics. In gatherings like FET, the best closings uplift each individual and deepen the sense of unity among the team members. The aim for the end of the gathering is to bring people more deeply into their hearts and remind each participant that their voice is as valued as the voice of the person next to them.

Since we have fit a lot into the ninety minutes of a FET meeting, there are usually only a few minutes left for closure. This is one reason we use our go-to question across nearly every FET team's first meeting: "What is one word or phrase that captures how you feel as we come to the end of our first FET gathering?" Another reason this is a reliably powerful closing activity is because it brings everyone's voice back into the room and together we form a collective poem that usually sounds something like "Connected . . . heard . . . motivated . . . not alone . . . inspired . . . ready for more."

It's beneficial to conclude the gathering with another sharing circle, in which each team member shares a word or a few sentences about how they feel, something they appreciate, or their hopes for next steps. For instance, at the close of one FET team's gathering in my district, we asked each person to share one word that captured how they felt in that moment. Parents used words such as *connected*, *hopeful*, *inspired*, and *content*. When it was the principal's turn, he said, "*Stretched*." I joked, "Another name for FET is *principal yoga*."

The final parent in the circle, an Argentinian mother and college professor, shared the most fitting word that gets at the essence of FET. "I am feeling the word *kurtum*," she said. "It comes from the Mapuche people in Patagonia. It means *to listen in order to be transformed*." No single word exists in English to capture this intention, but her seven words capture the spirit of FET precisely.

Nine parents, eight staff members, and a handful of students attended our inaugural in-person FET meeting at Louisville Middle School in September 2021. While the meeting's outdoor setting was inviting, it was clear that everyone was feeling nervous. Educators and family members sat clustered together eating their tacos on opposite sides of the patio. Fortunately, the co-leader, Brian, a much-loved Spanish teacher, used humor to break the ice. As he initiated the opening circle, he asked everyone to share their name, their child's name, and one word that captured what led them to join the team. When the first two parents to speak shared several sentences, Brian teasingly said, "That was more like thirty-five words for those of you counting!"

The team engaged in a quick team-builder and then shifted to a brief presentation by a community partner that focused on reducing the digital divide for Spanish-speaking families. At the meeting's halfway point, we arrived at the heart of what FET is all about—dialogue that builds trust, a collaborative spirit, and an orientation toward action. It emerged in a very organic way.

Brian asked participants what was on their minds and what they wanted to be the focus of their second meeting. When Brian's query was met with silence, a parent leader who had participated years earlier on another school's FET team asked the other families, "What do you need from the school? What would be helpful?" One at a time, parents spoke up.

"I want to know if there are still help sessions before school." This first question sparked the kind of conversation that FET was designed for.

"We have that information on our website," one of the staff members responded. She turned to confirm with the principal, and he nodded.

"I don't know if we update that information, though, so that it's current," chimed in another teacher.

"I am pretty sure that none of us use the school website," the mother responded.

This relatively small aspect of the school's operations exemplified a much larger issue: a persistent communication gap between the school and Spanish-speaking families. Families were not receiving needed information because the staff were using a one-dimensional approach to communication. Might the absence of Latino students in before- and after-school academic support offerings be contributing to achievement and opportunity gaps? Absolutely.

Another parent then jumped in, "If I would like to meet with a teacher, can I get an interpreter? Am I able to walk in and meet with the teacher right away, or do I need to schedule it?"

These great questions helped the school begin to uncover barriers that had been there for decades. The seeds of potential projects were already emerging:

- A FAQ document, in both printed and virtual forms, with questions that parents on the team could generate and also make suggestions for potential answers
- A staff directory with bilingual educators starred so families know whom to reach out to
- An app that would allow families and educators to communicate more easily with each other across language barriers
- An easy-to-access source of information on before-school help sessions

The meeting ended as FET teams often do, with every participant having an equal voice, sharing a few words that captured how they felt as the gathering concluded. What they said illustrates why FET is needed in so many of our schools.

The first parent to speak said, "I have six children, and they've been coming to this school for many years. I never would come to meetings before because they were always in English, and I didn't feel comfortable. These meetings are in my language, and I feel heard."

In the final moments, several more voices came forth with words like *unity*, *trust*, *community*, and *gratitude*. They had a clear road map for the months ahead, one that they would forge together. Everyone left feeling connected and uplifted, and the staff's perspective had been expanded by voices that they weren't used to hearing. Parents took on leadership roles for the next meeting, such as notetaker, communicator, and meal planner.

After the meeting ended, Brian walked up to me and thanked me for pushing him to lead the meeting in Spanish. Having the meeting held in their language of comfort was immeasurably important to families—practically, symbolically, and emotionally. Brian worked closely with two parents between that first meeting and the following one to make sure the answers for the FAQ document were written in a way that would most resonate with families. The document would be refined over the course of the year, sent via text to families, and ultimately mailed to all Spanish-speaking families the following summer.

Conclusion

First impressions matter. It can be hard to recover from a weak first FET meeting. Conversely, a strong start can build momentum throughout the school year, so taking the meeting and agenda planning process seriously is essential to ensuring that your initial FET gathering flourishes. As we have seen in this chapter, setting the stage for a highly effective first FET meeting requires attention to detail and significant work on the front end.

While most teams will have a successful and compelling launch meeting, we can still learn valuable lessons from the occasional school that struggles. What is missing from these gatherings and the choices made or not made by team leaders can illuminate why certain elements of an effective FET meeting are so important.

Even though premeeting preparation is necessary, it is not sufficient. Equally important is the unique set of leadership skills required to achieve FET's objectives. In the next chapter, we will turn to the qualities and actions of great team leaders.

Questions for Reflection and Discussion

1. As you reflect on the key elements of an effective FET team meeting, what surprised you or felt most useful?

2. What are a few ways that team leaders can foster psychological safety so that both family members and educators can engage authentically?

3. As you reflect on the elements of a strong meeting, which parts would you feel confident about leading, and where might you need to bolster your skill set?

4. What tasks or roles, if any, do you want to delegate to team members before, during, or after the first team meeting?

5. As you prepare for your first FET gathering, what are you most excited about, and what do you feel most concerned about? What lingering questions do you have?

CHAPTER 5

Being a Great Team Leader

Not all of us can do great things.
But we can do small things with great love.

—Mother Teresa

Of the many factors that support a thriving FET team, one stands out: *leadership*. Dedicated and thoughtful leaders can make all the difference. They help their team build momentum and keep it. They accomplish this by building strong rapport with team members, demonstrating follow-through, and maintaining strong communication with all stakeholders.

In this chapter, we will explore in some depth what it means to be an excellent leader and facilitator and examine these through ten leadership stances. We will also explore some big-picture leadership strategies that increase the likelihood of success with action projects that emerge in FET and other school-family partnership efforts.

Leaders as Facilitators

In many initial FET gatherings, team members are hesitant to share openly due to a lack of trust or because the school culture does not welcome constructive feedback from either staff or families. As a result, FET meetings can easily veer into team members sharing either general comments or overwhelmingly positive remarks on existing conditions. For FET gatherings to become spaces for heartfelt conversations and steady transformation—for both the individual participants and the overarching culture of the school—team leaders must become increasingly masterful in their facilitation.

However, even when FET leaders naturally possess some of these attributes or skill sets, it does not guarantee success. Facilitating groups of adults is complex and at times intimidating. In FET, the time pressure of only having ninety minutes once a month is undeniable. There are also a host of nuances when leading a group that must navigate cross-cultural differences, various power dynamics, and ingrained ways of interacting that are often invisible but impact everyone. If team leaders embody these approaches, they will be off to a great start, but leadership of a dynamic team such as FET requires developing more robust facilitation skills over time.

Early in my teaching career, while co-leading weekend SEL workshops for educators and school leaders, I experienced the challenge of being an effective facilitator. I was often unsure about what moves to make, even with a detailed agenda, and I regularly reflected on missteps that offered insight into how to maximize engagement and group cohesion. When facilitating meetings that involved significant power differentials, I wasn't sure how to encourage those with less authority to share their thoughts freely. When the quality of the group's connection or the achievement of the outcomes fell short of the potential, I sometimes couldn't figure out where or why we had faltered. After fifteen years of cofacilitating trainings, I still wrestled with doubt and insecurity.

From my experiences with students, I knew that I wanted to be a facilitator of learning rather than a "sage on the stage." However, I did not know what that looked like with a group of adults who had not signed on to learn from me. Should I guide the group or get out of their way?

The root of the word *facilitator* is the Latin word *facilis*, which means *easy to do* (Facilitate, n.d.). I realized that my goal, regardless of setting, was to make it easier for participants to be their authentic selves and fully engage. But what is the best way to guide groups with ease, and help other facilitators do so—particularly in settings such as FET where educators must guide meetings across significant racial, cultural, linguistic, and power differences? Regardless of good intentions, these educators are often representatives of the groups that continue to hold the most power in our public education system: White, American, native English speakers.

To further compound the challenge, many FET leaders are both teachers *and* team leaders. They often face the prospect of leading a team that includes many of their peers. Even more intimidating, they must lead FET gatherings in front of their boss, and are tasked with the high-stakes, dynamic work of leading a diverse team despite usually being a beginning facilitator.

All these factors contributed to my intention in 2018 to deepen my skill set as a facilitator and coach of other facilitators. As fate would have it, the previous year I had joined my wife's Zen community, which was led by Diane Musho Hamilton. In addition to being an outstanding Zen teacher, Diane is an esteemed facilitator and the author of such books as *Everything Is Workable* (Hamilton, 2013) and *Compassionate Conversations* (Hamilton, Wilson, & Loh, 2020). Diane's teachings and my experience in the Zen community heavily influenced my understanding of leadership.

Ten FET Leadership Stances

From that learning experience, two decades of my own facilitation journey, and the wisdom from research and dozens of books on leadership, here are ten of my greatest learnings about leadership and group facilitation.

1. Be clear about intentions.
2. Listen deeply.
3. Ask great questions.
4. Know your role.
5. Take a relational approach.
6. Serve as a connector.
7. Track individual and group energy.
8. Demonstrate flexibility and responsiveness.
9. View self as instrument.
10. Learn from other leaders.

Be Clear About Intentions

An effective facilitator has tremendous clarity about their intentions and conveys them transparently. As Diane teaches, "intention drives attention" (D. Hamilton, personal communication, April 3, 2019). A strong facilitator helps the group clarify the overriding intentions for the gathering. In moments as a facilitator when big decisions are required, it is important to prioritize two questions:

1. What is my intention?
2. What is the group's intention?

Let your intention drive your attention to what you privilege. "We often choose the template—and the activities and structure that go along with it—before we're clear on our purpose," writes Parker (2018, p. 4) in *The Art of Gathering*. "Make purpose your bouncer. Let it decide what goes into your gathering and what stays out" (Parker, 2018, p. 32). Great facilitators balance openness and attunement to the group's needs with intentionality.

As we've explored in other chapters, there are moments in FET gatherings when it serves the team to shift directions. There are also many moments when team leaders make the more difficult move: kindly acknowledging a team member whose comment or question is pulling the team off track, and pivoting back to what holds most meaning for the whole team. This might sound like the facilitator saying to an individual, "I appreciate you sharing your perspective. We now need to shift to the next item on our agenda so that we can maintain our momentum." Or "Thanks for saying that. We'll make sure to revisit that topic at our next meeting."

For families and time-squeezed educators alike, schools have rarely created space for people's stories, concerns, and innovative ideas to be heard. As a result, it is very possible that an individual participant might unintentionally or consciously hijack the agenda to share an adverse experience. FET is the right place for these perspectives to emerge, but they need to be contained within the structure put forth by the team leaders. In doing so, all participants can feel that the team leaders are honoring what led them to attend while protecting them from the whims of any given individual.

Listen Deeply

All people want to feel heard. Great leaders continue to develop their capacity to listen deeply. Deep listening builds a sense of sameness, calms the nervous system, and transforms us, as we drop the "I" reference point and try to see things through a new perspective. Deep listening is distinct from our typical approach to listening in that we:

- Give our full attention by avoiding multitasking or thinking about our response
- Read cues from people's body language, in recognition of the fact that 93 percent of communication is nonverbal (Miller-Muro, 2023)
- Face the speaker, make steady eye contact, and show an awareness of our own body language
- Tune in to what people are saying and not saying in their comments, to gain insight and spark new inquiries
- Use reflective listening techniques, such as summarizing, synthesizing, or acknowledging an impactful phrase or sentence when the speaker finishes sharing
- Ask questions to clarify or affirm an individual's comment or take the conversation deeper
- Listen with an open heart and a willingness to be transformed

In our schools, underrepresented families often don't feel heard (Mapp et al., 2022). Sometimes that is because traditional school events ask parents to primarily listen. Whether it is back-to-school night or parent-teacher conferences, the typical setup is for the educators to talk extensively and, if time permits, families can ask a few questions. This serves to perpetuate the dynamic of educator as expert and parent as passive recipient of information (Mapp et al., 2022).

In most schools, there is rarely the intentional effort for staff to ask questions and treat the families as experts on their children (Santana et al., 2016). This is part of what makes FET so unique and powerful: each gathering is centered on a few carefully selected questions that are intended to solicit parent experiences and insights. Educators learn quickly with FET that deep listening is the pathway both to changing their own individual approach with families and to helping the school transform its culture.

All team members become more candid in their sharing when they realize their experiences will not be dismissed or judged. "As *our listening* becomes more open—and speakers start to trust that they are being heard by people whose only desire is to make it safe for everyone to tell the truth—*their speaking* becomes more open as well," writes Palmer (2004, p. 120).

Ask Great Questions

Ask great questions. It sounds simple enough, but if we're honest, most of us are more focused on sounding smart in our answers or comments. Questions can be like "lanterns," illuminating new possibilities for partnership and collaboration (O'Donohue,

2018, p. 6). The quality of FET gatherings is often shaped by the quality of our questions. Thoughtful and thought-provoking questions reveal our openness to other perspectives, show that we truly value others, and communicate respect and interest.

Since great questions emerge from sincere curiosity, as you listen deeply, try to pay attention to what intrigues you or sparks wonder. Ask follow-up questions that energize the group, lead participants to share in greater depth, or take the conversation deeper. The best questions tend to:

- Be open ended
- Come from a mindset of not already knowing the right answer
- Be grounded in a genuine desire to learn
- Expand rather than restrict the arena of exploration (Palmer, 2004)
- Be provocative by interrupting the person's thinking and causing disequilibrium (Campbell Jones et al., 2020)
- Evoke passion (Campbell Jones et al., 2020)

In appendix D (page 147) you will find an extensive list of questions you can use with team members to foster connections and deepen understanding.

During a meeting of team leaders, a FET leader shared the biggest facilitation lesson they learned from their FET leadership experience:

> Ask questions in different ways, and provide different and multiple opportunities to answer them. Some of our community members have different comfort levels with speaking and sharing, so we need to be patient and flexible in supporting each participant's personal road toward belonging.

It is also valuable to model great questions for both parents and colleagues. This allows participants to experience and then attempt questions that prompt deeper conversations. A great book that goes into depth on how to do this effectively is *Partnering With Parents to Ask the Right Questions*. Authors Luz Santana and colleagues (2016) remind us that "the ability to ask questions is not only a sophisticated thinking skill but also an essential advocacy one" (p. 7).

In FET, the right question can unleash storytelling that both provides great insights about existing challenges and helps everyone see that apparently intractable issues can be transformed. At the beginning of a FET meeting at an elementary school, we had a warm-up question that was not related to our central goals for the evening. We asked parents to talk with a partner about the following question: "In terms of communication, what is something that a teacher has done in the past that you have really valued?"

>>>

While there were only four parents in attendance that night, the common theme that emerged shed light on an underused strategy. Three of the four parents said that they deeply appreciated when teachers at their previous schools texted them a photograph of their child engaged in a classroom activity. One mother was so enthusiastic about this strategy that she immediately showed us a photograph, accompanied by a brief description of what her son was doing. These ten minutes of sharing revealed a best practice that most teachers at the school could easily implement.

Know Your Role

To be effective, all team leaders need to be clear on what their role is as facilitator. This definition can be fluid depending on the needs of the group, the context, and the desired outcomes. I like Parker's (2018) definition that a facilitator "is someone trained in the skill of shaping group dynamics and collective conversations" (p. xi). Some of the responsibilities of an effective facilitator are to:

- Bring out everyone's best
- Serve and achieve the outcomes needed for the group
- Harness individual and collective energy
- Honor people's contributions
- Help the group as a whole and each individual feel safe to be authentic
- Be both penetrative and receptive
- Bring forth their and others' full range of humanity

How do we bring forth others' full range of humanity? Accomplishing this is particularly important in spaces like FET where our aim is to create transformation and challenge the status quo. We do so by making the space safe for the soul to emerge, which is perhaps the greatest challenge any facilitator faces.

Palmer (2004) reminds us that facilitators "must understand the solemn responsibility that accompanies a work in which people are invited to make their souls vulnerable and promised that they will be done no harm" (p. 77). FET leaders know instinctively or learn from missed opportunities that an effective way to build or deepen trust is to bring their own vulnerability first or affirm the first courageous parent or educator to do so.

While FET leaders do not typically call on specific team members to speak, another way to create safety and gently invite broader participation is to draw in people who are reserved by saying something like "Roberta, we haven't heard from you. Is there anything that you'd like to contribute?" Two other effective ways to bring in quieter voices are to give participants regular opportunities to talk in small groups or share in order around the circle. This provides introverts and others who might feel reticent the opportunity to contribute to the conversation without needing to interject. If participants always have the right to pass when it's their turn in the circle, they will feel even more relaxed.

Team leaders also might ask a colleague to privately capture data on who speaks and how many times they verbally participate, a strategy that I learned in trainings on Socratic seminars. Over time, this helps us create more balanced participation and prevent the same people from always dominating the conversation. This is the work of the participant tracker, one of the team roles described in the Define FET Team Roles section of chapter 2 (page 31).

It is also crucial as facilitators of diverse spaces to be attuned to how the powerful and privileged are affecting the conversation and how the marginalized are being impacted. In FET, we consistently use structures that make space for marginalized voices, such as timed dyads or sharing circles that give all participants a chance to share their perspective.

I have learned from Diane and other mentors that while our efforts as facilitators matter, we also want to hold ourselves lightly and guide any group with humility. This includes being comfortable with not knowing the answer or the right next step, as well as consistently drawing out the wisdom of the group.

A final component of knowing your role as facilitator is demonstrating an awareness that you're not supposed to do everything. Educators can have a hard time letting go of control. However, educators also learn over time that they become more effective when they distribute leadership and empower students with greater responsibility. In that spirit, strong facilitators of FET realize that they don't have to play every role, and remember to delegate responsibilities to team members. More about this, and a helpful list of roles to delegate, can be found in chapter 4 (page 59).

Take a Relational Approach

Facilitators need to be cautious of reducing meetings to a transactional approach, particularly in settings that have historically marginalized certain voices and are striving to change existing paradigms. One of the main reasons we struggle to make progress in creating more equitable systems is a lack of relationships (Mapp et al., 2022). For relationships to flourish, it is crucial that facilitators are intentional about devising structures that foster psychological safety for each individual *and* foster group unity.

In the early years of FET, I learned that if we jumped straight into group conversation, both families and staff were often reluctant to share. This is the reason FET meetings begin with mealtimes, team-builders, and opening circles. These are essential and foundational activities to any successful FET gathering. This approach honors the wisdom of the adage, *Go slow to go fast*. To accomplish this, facilitators need to ensure that strengthening relationships is the priority. In a meeting, this translates to focusing as much on building connections and relating to each other as on discussing topics (Mapp et al., 2022). People come first, before the process and the goals. Teams accelerate their progress when there is a foundation of strong relationships and trust.

Serve as a Connector

It is important that team leaders are skilled not just at building relationships with participants but also at cultivating relationships between them. While the facilitator needs to hold the whole—prioritizing what will benefit the group more than what might serve individual needs—it is also important for the facilitator to pay attention to and connect with the individuals in the group. When many of us see a group, we feel a group, not individuals (D. Hamilton, personal communication, April 2, 2019). Team leaders need to attune to who is relaxed, who is eager, who is checked out, who is hostile, and so on.

The FET leaders who most effectively strengthen rapport or pivot mid-meeting track the body language and facial expressions of individual participants. They also fortify connections with team members that they don't know well by holding conversations with them before and after gatherings. This ultimately strengthens the whole team.

Team leaders also need to see themselves as bridges that help individuals connect with each other and not solely with them or the group as a whole. As Parker (2018) writes, "One measure of a successful gathering is that it starts off with a higher number of host-guest connections than guest-guest and ends with those tallies reversed, far in the guest-guest favor" (p. 92).

FET leaders should be intentional about connecting family members with other families and building opportunities for parents to comfortably interact with educators. One of the most effective ways they can accomplish this is by providing multiple opportunities for participants to talk with a partner or in a small group. Another way to achieve this weaving of individuals is by honoring and synthesizing what participants have expressed, such as "What you just shared connects to what Roberta said a few minutes ago."

A final way to create stronger ties between individuals is to foster cross talk, which means that the facilitator does not always alternate with the most recent speaker. In many school gatherings, it is quite common for a ping-pong effect to occur in which the leader invites a question or comment and then feels obliged to respond immediately afterward. This back-and-forth prevents any flow from one team member's voice to another. One strategy to work around this pattern is to set up a "stack" in which you state the names of the next few people who have volunteered to speak, and you only interject a comment between their consecutive comments if it's something that is vital to enhancing the conversation.

Track Individual and Group Energy

Great facilitators respond to the energy in the space and adjust accordingly, as well as work to shift the energy to heighten levels of both individual and collective engagement. Facilitators need to track and assess the subtle energy in the group and not simply attend to the content of what is being said. It's like when you are in a car with someone who is angry—you can't see the anger but you sure can feel it. Subtle energy is felt but can't be measured easily. It is not always visible, although sometimes it can be reflected in people's body language or facial expressions (D. Hamilton, personal communication,

April 4, 2019). A strong facilitator has an accurate read of both individual and group energy, and then trusts their instincts in making the next move. When the facilitators fail to embody this approach, the whole team's energy and momentum can be derailed. Some ways to track and shift the energy in the group include the following.

- Pause at the door when you enter a group session as a reminder to tap into your subtle sensing capacity. While exhaling, gently release any thoughts you have been carrying and open your senses to the greater field of energy. Breathe in and notice what comes up (D. Hamilton, personal communication, April 3, 2019).

- Observe participants' body language, particularly their facial expressions and posture.

- As people share verbally, pay attention to whether their energy is invigorated or flat, and how other participants are responding (for example, are they turning to the speaker, leaning forward, or looking upward to reveal possible disengagement?).

- Share observations about what you notice (for example, "It seems like a lot of people's energy just dipped; let's shift gears").

- Move people's energy in the direction that you want to see, which could look like asking a question that will galvanize enthusiasm or shifting the agenda (for example, moving into small-group conversations sooner than planned).

- Be more playful. Playfulness as a form of adult expression allows us to be more fully expressive, daring, and connected.

- Rouse participants' energy by getting their bodies involved, even in simple ways such as saying, "Raise your hand if you agree . . ."

- Be a disrupter by bringing forth a challenge, which brings more wakeful energy and leads people to greater presence.

As Senge (2000) writes, "In the practice of dialogue, we pay attention not only to the words but to the spaces between the words. . . . Not only to the things people say but to the timbre and tones of their voices" (p. 75). Many groups are so focused on content and completing agenda items that they do not work in the subtle realm. As a result, these groups tend to be far less efficient, joyful, and creative (D. Hamilton, personal communication, April 3, 2019).

When the energy in the group is stagnant, it can be effective for the facilitator to step back from the group and be a disrupter. Sometimes this means saying the things that aren't being said or challenging the group.

Demonstrate Flexibility and Responsiveness

It's challenging to stay fully present as a facilitator. This might happen because we're planning our next move or are stuck in our thoughts because of something that just occurred. However, as facilitators, we are at our best when we are relaxed and responsive. We thrive when we are able to let go of our own concerns and tune in to what is happening around us.

"I have a tendency to want to stick to the plan," one FET leader shared at our final quarterly gathering of team leaders. "This past year I've learned the value of listening and the power in flexibility." FET leaders are more fluid and skillful in their facilitation when they arrive at meetings well prepared, have clarity about their intentions, and know in advance what aspects of the agenda they are open to modifying or skipping. If someone brings up a timely topic or makes a compelling comment, they are able shift gears and make space for what matters most to the group. FET team leaders can demonstrate their flexibility by giving more time to a part of the agenda than they originally allotted because it has sparked passionate participation. They can show responsiveness by saying, "We'll add that to next month's agenda since there is clearly interest in going deeper into this topic."

I saw this in action at one middle school FET gathering. During the quick updates section of the meeting, the principal briefly shared the benefits of students taking the state tests instead of opting out. We allotted three minutes for the principal to share this information and take a question or two. However, the thirty-two parents in attendance were curious why the test mattered, which sparked a rich forty-five-minute conversation about achievement and opportunity gaps. This shift prompted the facilitators to scrap their intended agenda. Two months later the principal reported back that student participation rates in testing were the highest in nearly a decade.

View Self as Instrument

A crucial step on the path to becoming a strong facilitator is to become more self-knowledgeable and self-aware. As we help guide a group, we are not just downloading tips and tools; we are bringing our own humanity into greater service and enacting more of who we are to strengthen our communities.

Becoming an effective facilitator means committing to significant and ongoing personal development and viewing "self as instrument" (D. Hamilton, personal communication, April 3, 2019). Research shows that the more developed a person becomes, the more self-awareness they have (Kegan & Lahey, 2016). The driving notion behind self as instrument is that we see ourselves as a powerful force for change. Like a musical instrument, we need to be optimally tuned, which means constantly refining ourselves. This requires taking a closer look at our strengths, weaknesses, and biases. For instance, this might look like asking a trusted colleague for feedback after a FET meeting or reflecting on what you did well and where you could improve.

The more specific your reflections can be, the better. For example, if there was an exchange where you felt like you missed the mark, you can revisit that moment in your mind's eye and ask yourself, "How was I feeling as I spoke?" or "What might have been a more effective response?" Another vital way to enhance your ongoing growth is to commit to continued learning, such as taking an online course or attending a retreat related to your holistic growth. Please note that I chose the word *holistic* instead of *professional* because sometimes the learning experiences that make us more comfortable in our skin have outsized benefits on our professional efficacy.

From square one with potential leaders, I acknowledge that FET is a small fraction of their life. I know that outside of the monthly planning sessions and quarterly FET leaders meeting, they will not have extensive time to "sharpen the saw" as Covey (2020, p. 371) describes continuous self-improvement efforts. For this reason, when I partner with principals around identifying potential FET leaders, we look for individuals who already demonstrate many of the FET leadership skills mentioned in this book.

It's also vital that FET leaders embody a growth mindset. This makes them flexible leaders who are open to improvement and receptive to constructive feedback, be it from families or colleagues. By being humble and approachable, they become the kind of leaders that teams need to do such dynamic cross-cultural work.

Learn From Other Leaders

It's important to create learning communities among FET leaders. Every FET team is different, faces its own challenges, and has its own strengths. Bringing team leaders from all FET schools together allows them to learn from each other and build cross-school connections. It also sparks insights for each leader to inform their team's next steps and enhance their own leadership skills. These team leaders' gatherings, as well as what team leaders can learn at planning sessions from the district lead from their experiences at other schools' meetings, can be invaluable.

In the final team leaders' meeting in the last month of the school year, focus on both celebrating teams' strides and synthesizing their leadership learnings. Before sharing verbally as a whole group, ask team members to answer several questions in the form of a survey that can become a shared document for them to discuss or reference in the future. Figure 5.1 (page 86) lists some of the questions you may ask them to reflect upon. The online reproducible of this figure also includes space at the bottom for you to add your own questions.

At that final meeting, it can also be beneficial to gift team leaders a book that will support their leadership or deepen their understanding of the kinds of partnerships FET strives to forge, such as *Just Schools: Building Equitable Collaborations With Families and Communities* by Ann Ishimaru (2020).

Team leader gatherings are valuable because they offer practical guidance and healthy doses of inspiration, and help team leaders feel that they are part of a movement—a larger *FETwork* of change agents that they can borrow ideas from or lean on for support.

In the spirit of learning from other leaders, I'd like to include the following list of advice from previous FET leaders.

- Don't leave out the team-builders or the food. They are essential.
- Always find a way to get everyone's voice in the room at every meeting. Pay attention to how much you are talking versus how much FET participants are talking.
- Personal phone invitations seem to be most effective for recruiting families.

End-of-Year Team Leader Reflection Questions

- What have you most enjoyed about co-leading FET? What has been challenging in your leadership experience?
- What have been some of your biggest learnings in terms of being an effective facilitator of FET gatherings? What questions do you still have about facilitation?
- Do you have any suggestions about how next year's four FET all-leaders gatherings could be more helpful or meaningful? What are some ways that your school can more intentionally build stronger relationships with all families?
- What strategies have you found most useful in terms of recruiting families to attend FET? What is most useful for recruiting staff?
- How has your understanding of FET shifted since the beginning of the year?
- What advice would you like to share with new FET leaders?
- What innovative ideas do you have about how to share what happens in FET with staff and families that do not attend FET?
- What do you notice in your school community that confirms that FET is making a difference?
- Is there anything else that you would like to share about how FET can grow stronger at your school?

Figure 5.1: Team leader reflection questions.

Visit **go.SolutionTree.com/diversityandequity** *for a free reproducible version of this figure.*

- Send the notes from each meeting to the entire staff and encourage them to read them, so that they can be aware of the work you are doing. Include an invitation to the next meeting.
- It's important to go with the flow of the conversation and not steer it back to the agenda when an important issue comes up. It's a good idea to know what you may want to cut from the agenda ahead of time because things often take longer than expected.
- We do not need to have an answer for everything; it is OK not to know, but just make sure to follow up.
- Delegating to others has been difficult, but I am getting better and it is necessary.
- Keep in mind how to have tangible outcomes from meetings that can become structural changes in your school.
- Keep your conversations directed toward what is within your immediate scope of control, what may need to include leadership, and what the team can self-organize.
- I have found that people respond to genuine care from the leaders, which has helped me to assume the role of both a leader and a listener.

- Listen to parents because no matter how long you have been an educator, you will learn *a lot*! It's really great to have a parent as a co-leader. They give a very valuable perspective!

- Write things down! It's hard to remember everything if you haven't taken notes.

- Parents need time to get comfortable participating. It's important to carefully think through each detail of the meeting so that parents feel welcome.

- Don't always look for a "big" win—often, it is little wins and changes that make a big difference.

- Having FET sewn into the fabric of your school culture is a good goal.

- Send thank-you letters to families for being there.

- The first couple of meetings are the trickiest. As the year goes on, it gets easier to plan, and the meetings start to feel very comfortable.

- Involve a parent to give feedback about what is working and not working at meetings.

Conclusion

The ten qualities of great FET leaders explored in this chapter show us how effective leaders play an instrumental role in ensuring that their teams thrive. In the next chapter, we'll explore how teams maintain momentum throughout the arc of the school year, navigate potential challenges, and continue to build trust and transform practices in their school community.

Questions for Reflection and Discussion

1. As you reflect on the ten leadership qualities, which surprised you or stood out to you?

2. What are your greatest strengths as a facilitator?

3. What facets of facilitation are you most trying to improve?

4. What concrete step or two can you take to improve your skill set in one of the ten areas?

5. In what aspects of leadership would you be wise to rely on your co-leader or co-leaders who have complementary strengths?

CHAPTER 6

Taking Action and Sustaining the Momentum

If you have come here to help me, you are wasting your time. But if you have come because your liberation is bound up with mine, then let us work together.
—Aboriginal Activist Group, Queensland, Australia

What all great teams strive for is praxis, which is putting reflection and learning into action. At its essence, "praxis compels people to bring their true selves to whatever they are doing because what they are doing is authentic" (Knight, 2022, p. 30). Paulo Freire, one of the first true educational reformers, considered praxis to be a revolutionary action, believing that it is "reflection and action upon the world in order to transform it" (as cited in Knight, 2022, p. 31).

The current reality is that most schools find it easier to continue doing events in the same ways that they have always done them. Rarely does the staff itself have the time, space, or encouragement to innovate, and much less with families sitting around the table offering insights. As Mapp and colleagues (2022) write about the current landscape of school-family engagement practices:

> Even in school gatherings that bring families together, the opportunities for parents to talk with each other are brief and infrequent. Within a typical school community, the casual nature of encounters with other families does not create relationships that parents consider trusting and meaningful. (p. 69)

For our schools to make the progress needed in our partnerships with families (and our approach to nearly every aspect of schooling), we need to demonstrate a willingness to "disrupt what's already in motion," refine existing practices, and innovate amid the reality that schools are one of the public institutions often most attached to maintaining the status quo (Ishimaru, 2020, p. 140).

In this chapter, we will take a closer look at action projects and how to ensure that your team's efforts help not only the FET members but also the school as a whole. Then we will explore several strategies, along with case studies, that strong teams consistently prioritize to preserve the FET momentum. After we explore these pathways to sustaining positive change, we will touch on what this means for leaders. We then finish by exploring some of the FET outcomes for all stakeholders.

Make the Most of Your Team's Action Projects

The action projects that FET teams devise and accomplish are the true engine for sparking meaningful change. They ensure that rich conversations at FET gatherings ripple out to positively impact more underrepresented families, staff, and the broader school community.

The following action projects have emerged from previous FET teams as natural next steps to strengthening communication and relationships and gradually transforming the quality of partnerships between staff and families:

- A FAQ document that helped families access vital information
- The powerful practice of staff engaging in relationship-centered home visits
- A parent panel that honored the voices of underrepresented families and supported an entire school staff's professional learning around strengthening partnerships with families
- The development of a staff-wide positive phone call system
- A school that completely reinvented their back-to-school night
- The implementation of a two-way communication app that dramatically improved communication across language barriers between staff and Spanish-speaking families
- A team that revamped parent-teacher conferences to make them more accessible for all

As you think about potential action projects that your school or district might focus on, I encourage you to use Mapp's (2021) four guiding questions for assessing an action step, as they align well with the spirit of FET:

1. Is this practice relational?
2. Does it treat families as valuable and equal partners?
3. Is it culturally responsive and respectful?
4. Is it collaborative and interactive?

After you and your team have identified an action project that fits these criteria, it will be helpful to develop a detailed plan for carrying out this initiative. You are much more likely to succeed if you determine key elements early on, such as who will primarily be responsible for carrying out specific parts of the project and what timeline seems feasible.

Figure 6.1 presents a planning guide that team leaders can use to help organize and determine the efficacy of a team's action projects.

Action Projects Planning Guide

School: _____   Date: _____

Team Leaders: _____

Action Project 1: _____

How will this project address the themes that have surfaced at team meetings?

What action steps will the FET team organize to support this project? Fill in the following table.

Action step	Completion date	Who will help accomplish this?	How will we determine the success of this action step?

Action Project 2: _____

How will this project address the themes that have surfaced at team meetings?

What action steps will the FET team organize to support this project? Fill in the following table.

Action step	Completion date	Who will help accomplish this?	How will we determine the success of this action step?

Figure 6.1: FET action projects planning guide.

*Visit **go.SolutionTree.com/diversityandequity** for a free reproducible version of this figure.*

When principals ask me about potential high-impact action projects that are easy to implement, I encourage them to focus their energy and their staff's limited bandwidth on one or two high-leverage school-family partnership practices, such as positive phone calls. The planning guide is helpful for FET teams and also a valuable tool for schools without FET because the absence of a team often results in too much responsibility landing on the principal or one staff member.

> The work of Louisville Middle School's team in its first year illustrates the value of creating space for families to feel heard, the fundamental importance of trust building, and what honest dialogue about existing gaps looks like in action. Louisville's FET team got off to a fast start when they created the FAQ document that emerged naturally out of their September meeting and gave families access to important information.
>
> However, it quickly became apparent how significant the relationship gap was between staff and Latino families. When only three parents attended the December meeting (compared to eleven at the September meeting), the team leaders and I carved out time to reflect on why we had lost momentum. I posited that the low turnout reflected an overall lack of relationship and trust between the staff and Spanish-speaking families, and the team leaders agreed.
>
> This insight led us to an unconventional action step: we canceled the January FET meeting and committed to engaging in home visits with the school's Latino families. I provided a brief training on home visits for staff members on the FET team, and they scheduled virtual visits (because they were still limited by COVID-19 restrictions).
>
> The staff came away from these visits with an array of insights. They asked parents about their hopes and dreams for their children, what they enjoyed doing outside of school, their strengths, and much more. Brian Gonzales, a co-leader of the team, said that engaging in the visits was the main reason it was the best January of his career. To top it off, when we returned for our February meeting, we had thirteen parents in attendance, including several families joining for the first time. Out of this meeting emerged a powerful action item: several Latino parent team leaders would record their perspectives and experiences for a virtual parent panel that staff would watch at a spring professional development session (Mapp et al., 2017).
>
> Since the parents' work schedules conflicted with them joining staff in person, Brian interviewed the three mothers and one father and showed the virtual panel to staff in mid-April. The four parents shared candidly about their experiences at the school and the extent to which language barriers were interfering with access to information and building relationships with staff. They said communication could be significantly improved, which could happen if teachers made the effort to translate their emails into Spanish or use an app to text with families.

An important outcome of FET is that we can help educators become more aware of their blind spots and biases, and the ways that those both individually and collectively erect barriers for underserved families. Some of them were surprised by "how much the families view language and culture as a barrier," and acknowledged that "parents appreciate the communication from school in their native language." Another teacher added, "I know that I don't communicate enough, and it's just because I get overwhelmed with all that comes with this job. I truly want to improve in this area! Parents deserve the best."

Staff members had several insights on both how to better connect with families and how to improve their teaching. Staff mentioned the need to "honor diversity among the Latino community." Several teachers also mentioned the "need to do more in terms of asking how the quiet or shy kids are doing and what they are understanding." The breadth of questions that Louisville's staff posed fueled our next conversations and gave us a road map for continued learning and direction as a team.

Preserve the FET Momentum

Now that you have learned how to start a FET team and support positive action projects, it's time to consider how you can keep the momentum going, accelerate your progress, and inspire similar positive change throughout your school and district. Let's explore the following seven strategies, some of which include illustrative case studies from FET teams.

1. Prioritize relationships and trust
2. Amplify parent voices
3. Identify existing barriers
4. Distinguish between change projects and family learning topics
5. Spark collaboration between team leaders and school leaders
6. Engage principals in annual reflection and visioning conversations
7. Create synergy with other school improvement efforts

Prioritize Relationships and Trust

When researchers studied the schools that were positive outliers during the first two years of the COVID-19 pandemic, a common thread between them was strong relationships (Kamenetz, 2022). When Mapp and colleagues (2022) looked closely at these schools, they found that educators "viewed relationship-building with families as the fundamental first step in establishing a positive culture at the school and ensuring student success" (p. 58).

The continuum in figure 6.2 shows the varying levels of impact of specific school-family engagement practices on student learning and makes clear that some of the best strategies for relationship building are also some of the most powerful ways to propel students' learning.

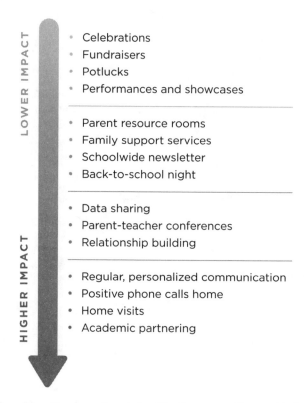

Source: © 2021 Adapted from Flamboyan Foundation, The Continuum of Impact. Used with permission.

Figure 6.2: The impact of family engagement strategies on student learning.

Amplify Parent Voices

One of the most effective ways to foster trust is to show families that we value their voices and want to genuinely listen to them. "Listening requires not only open eyes and ears, but open hearts and minds," Lisa Delpit (1995, p. 46) reminds us.

When we provide multiple opportunities at each FET meeting for parents to bring their voices, they grow increasingly comfortable and confident. This enables them to share their perspectives more candidly at future meetings when it is time to shift from connection to collaboration. As author Liz Fosslien (2022) puts it, "Diversity is having a seat at the table. Inclusion is having a voice. Belonging is having that voice heard."

Case Study: Mesa Elementary School

Mesa Elementary is a small school, with fewer than three hundred students, and White students make up more than 90 percent of the student population. As a result, nondominant families have often felt marginalized. With Mesa's team being brand new and every staff member on the team and the parent leader being White, I knew from the first meeting in September that we would need to be particularly intentional about building a trusting space. Parents of color needed to feel truly heard and understand that we genuinely wanted their input to spark concrete changes that would benefit them and their children.

In October, we had four parents in attendance, all of whom had gone to school outside of the United States in Argentina, Belgium, Brazil, and Mexico. We focused on providing them with multiple opportunities to have their voices heard. In the opening circle, we asked each person to share what drew them to FET and one or two things that were different between Mesa and schools in the country where they grew up. For the bulk of our meeting, we had a free-flowing conversation based on three questions:

1. What may be some of the challenges or barriers that multilingual or underrepresented families are grappling with at Mesa?

2. How can we help families feel more connected to their child's classroom, teacher, and school, particularly in this time where parents are not allowed to be in the building (due to COVID-19 restrictions)?

3. How could we, in creative ways, enhance two-way communication between families and staff?

After a rich conversation about these questions, we asked the parents to share their hopes in a word or two for what might unfold in our team in the months ahead. In November, the focus again was on centering parent voices and conveying how much we valued their input and feedback. We knew that in December we would shift our focus to identifying action items.

At the beginning of the December meeting, after the team-builder and opening circle, the parent leader explicitly stated, "We have three aims tonight: (1) continue to build trust and connection, (2) center your voices as parents and hear perspectives on what can be improved here at Mesa, and (3) begin identifying what we want to focus on as next steps or team goals." The bulk of the meeting focused on soliciting their feedback on the parent-teacher conferences that had just taken place, as well as how to make the Fall Festival more appealing, engaging, and relational for all families. We then spent the remaining time discussing how we could create a more inclusive environment at Mesa.

As we neared the close of the meeting, one mother said, "I'm really appreciating the space you've created here for us and the connections that are being built, but I'm all about action. I need to see changes happening to stay invested in this. When are we going to start talking about specifics?"

I responded, "Your timing is perfect. The focus of our next meeting is going to be all about identifying a couple specific initiatives that you all think would create the most meaningful change here at Mesa." While various ideas had surfaced in the November and December gatherings, it was time to narrow our focus as a team and select our change projects, which is exactly what we accomplished at the January meeting.

Identify Existing Barriers

In many schools, the inequities and barriers that underrepresented families confront are not addressed. This happens for three major reasons: (1) staff are unaware of the barriers that nondominant families experience, (2) families are not comfortable enough to share this constructive feedback with staff, and (3) the school never creates the space or solicits the feedback that would illuminate the broken systems or missed opportunities. Particularly at schools where underrepresented students comprise a small minority of the overall school population, their families can often feel voiceless and even invisible.

Case Study: Eisenhower Elementary School

When a FET team was launched at Eisenhower Elementary, a school in which Latino students make up less than 10 percent of the student population, families had long felt on the margins. Even though we asked benign questions at the first FET gathering, such as "What is going well so far for your child?" parents hardly spoke in our whole-group conversation.

In response, the team leaders and I designed a second meeting that provided ample time for team members to meet in groups of three to discuss the positive and challenging experiences they or their children had experienced thus far in the school year. What parents shared when we returned to the larger circle made it clear that communication and relationships between most teachers and Latino families were nonexistent.

"I haven't met or talked with my child's teacher," one mother said.

"I have not received any communication from our teacher," another mother commented.

"I don't know my child's teacher's name, and didn't know it last year either," added a third.

A quick show of hands revealed that eight out of ten parents had not had a single connection with their child's teacher, and all of them said they had not received any communication. Research has shown "the lack of, quality of, and clarity of communication" is one of the largest barriers for families to engage with their children's schools (Mapp et al., 2022, p. 72). I felt both disheartened and motivated by parents' comments and moved the conversation along quickly so that staff did not have time to feel defensive or embarrassed.

From this discussion, our first action step naturally emerged: training staff on implementing the TalkingPoints app that allowed for two-way communication via text and translated messages into the preferred language of the user. We had ten teachers pilot use of the app.

Later in the year, when we asked parents to share what they felt proud of that our team accomplished in its first year, one father reflected:

> Teachers using the TalkingPoints app happened because of our meetings. I'm now seeing the impact, especially for the parents that can't communicate easily in English. It is now super easy; parents and teachers don't have excuses anymore. When other parents send

a text, they are happily shocked—"Yes, they do respond!" Now the teacher's name is right there on my phone, and we can text any time. Many things have changed at the school—relationships with teachers, communication, everything.

At the third meeting, we knew that the best way to deepen participants' sense of psychological safety and trust was to continue using small-group conversations. We had one group focus on what both families and staff needed for an effective implementation of TalkingPoints. A second group reflected on how parent-teacher conferences went and how they could be improved. A third group generated a list of topics that they would like to learn more about at a future FET meeting.

I happened to facilitate the small group that led to our next action project: revamping parent-teacher conferences. As a staff member and I listened, the three parents in our group shared that they had felt rushed and dominated by teacher talk. They also wished, as one father put it, that teachers would take the time to "ask about what our life is like at home and what we know about our child."

Within minutes, with chart paper in hand, the five of us generated a few concrete action steps that would be implemented before the next round of conferences.

- Conferences for families that utilized an interpreter would increase from twenty to thirty minutes. Since interpretation absorbs half of the designated time, this shift would make conferences more equitable for families that spoke a language other than English and provide staff with more time to hear from families.

- All staff would receive a professional development session on how to create a more culturally responsive and relationship-centered conference that included important questions to ask families and more time for staff to learn from and listen to parents. (As the trainer for this session, I was able to incorporate notes from these parents' insights as they shared with me what topics they most wanted addressed during their conference.)

- Families would receive a list of sample questions they could ask during conferences so that they could feel better prepared and find more meaning in the conversations.

We had to wait four months until the second and final round of parent-teacher conferences to know if these efforts had made any noticeable difference for families. When we asked about their experience with the second round of conferences, one parent started us off by saying, "We could talk more, we had more time to ask questions, and there was greater clarity between the two of us about my child's academic progress, behavior, and homework."

At the end of the year, I sat down with the principal to reflect on the team's first year and visions for the future. "FET has been an amazing thing," he said. "I couldn't have done it on my own. I don't have the resources or expertise to know how to do this. It has been a dream come true for me. I'm getting out of it exactly what I wanted—how to engage all my communities. Their feedback has been so helpful."

He also had some specific feedback on the results of our action projects:

> I just received the annual results of our parent survey. It's off the charts! I've been principal here for more than a decade, and we were always slightly ahead of the district average. This year we had massive gains compared to every other year. It was 3.74 [out of a maximum score of 4.0] compared to the district average, 3.2. And one of the biggest jumps in the data was around parent-teacher conferences. I made it a point to share that data with the staff the other day. I knew going in that some staff were reluctant to change their approach or give more time, but I've heard more positive talk about your training and the shifts we made with conferences than almost anything we've done this year. (B. Stroup, personal communication, April 27, 2022)

Distinguish Between Change Projects and Family Learning Topics

In my experience as a district leader, I have become adamant about every FET team having at least one concrete action project. This is because, in the early years, some FET teams reached the end of the school year and had not tangibly changed how the staff partnered with families. For teams to successfully complete their action projects, I have found that the second, third, and fourth monthly FET gatherings of the year are critical for unearthing barriers and identifying action steps.

If teams do not develop this clarity until the second half of the school year, they often fail to implement their action projects before the end of the school year. In shaping the agendas for the third and fourth meetings of the year, we are intentional about asking families and educators how we might create systemic change.

Case Study: Angevine Middle School

At the Angevine Middle School November meeting, following up on families sharing at the first meeting that they had not received any positive communication from staff, we put forth a positive phone call system as a prospective action project. We proposed that ten teachers pilot the TalkingPoints app.

Parallel to this process of identifying their change initiatives, we asked families what they would like to learn more about at future meetings. At Angevine, families conveyed that they wanted to learn more about after-school opportunities, resources in the community, mental health supports, and the school's approach to bullying and conflict resolution. Once we created this list, we asked team members to vote on their top three. This helped us determine both the themes for our learning time and the guest speakers that we would invite to Angevine's FET meetings in the second half of the year.

During the sixth year of FET, I began presenting annually to the superintendent and upper district leadership on the major themes that teams had uncovered and their action projects. While this January check-in was valuable to inform them of teams' efforts, by the second year of this tradition I realized it had a much larger benefit.

By asking team leaders to capture major themes and action projects in two succinct lists, it pushed them to get clear on their top priorities in terms of action steps in time for the second half of the school year. I also share these lists with the principals at all FET schools, which increases team leaders' motivation to do an outstanding job in articulately capturing their efforts.

Completing these lists also reveals the schools that are over-focused on parent learning opportunities and have not yet identified an action project. For instance, one of our high school teams listed two action steps. First, they wanted to "provide a short training for parents on Infinite Campus," which is the digital platform that enables families to check their student's attendance, grades, and so on. Second, they proposed "offering English language classes for parents." During our planning sessions, we affirmed that both of these steps would be extremely beneficial for families' learning. But stating them clearly in writing prompted the team leaders to identify actual projects, such as a pilot of the TalkingPoints app and reinventing back-to-school night to make it more relationship focused.

I believe that team leaders put their initial energy more toward parent learning for two major reasons. First, they know how hard it will be for the staff to start a new initiative when they are typically overwhelmed by all the existing initiatives. Second, they know instinctively it will be easier to coordinate learning presentations than collaborate with the staff in implementing systemic change.

Both carrying out action projects and deepening families' learning are vital assignments for any FET team. However, the action projects are the only one of these aims that create systemic change and have a notable impact on the quality of partnership between staff and families. One of the most common mistakes that I have seen many FET leaders make is they conflate the two. While family learning time equips them with valuable information, it does not change the way that parents engage with staff or vice versa.

Spark Collaboration Between Team Leaders and School Leaders

Achieving most action projects requires collaboration with principals and subsequent buy-in from the broader staff. As such, once a team gains clarity on their priorities by the third or fourth meeting, the team leaders and district lead should secure twenty to thirty minutes to meet with the school principal before the beginning of the second semester. During this conversation, the team leaders and district lead strategize with the principal on the specific aims of the project and an appropriate timeline. These aspirations should be ambitious yet realistic. Knowing that principals thoughtfully protect their staff from overwhelm, FET leaders engage in a meaningful back-and-forth with them to find the sweet spot between setting expectations too low and pushing too hard and fast.

For example, in one of these meetings, a principal told us that it was feasible to get ten to fifteen staff members piloting the TalkingPoints app by January. She committed to emailing staff immediately to gauge how many teachers were already using the app or interested in doing so. The principal also agreed to set aside ten minutes at their next faculty meeting to discuss implementation.

While team leaders can spark interest among colleagues in action projects through one-on-one conversations, they accelerate progress and create greater leverage when they collaborate with their principal. By engaging the principal in a short yet pivotal meeting before the second half of the school year begins, the district lead and the team leaders help set in motion a concrete plan that ensures positive changes are on the near horizon.

The first three meetings of the second half of the year then serve as the time for devising the details, soliciting final input from the team, starting implementation, and making refinements. This ensures that teams can devote the final two FET gatherings to reflection, celebration, and visioning.

Engage Principals in Annual Reflection and Visioning Conversations

Another powerful strategy for accelerating progress is to bring the district lead and FET principal together for an annual one-on-one conversation. These meetings should typically be held in April to avoid trying to connect with principals during the hectic final weeks of the school year. This approximately forty-five-minute check-in provides the opportunity for the principal and district lead to reflect on how the year went—celebrating accomplishments, identifying lessons, and visioning forward. It affirms principals' commitment, honors the impact they have had on the teams' progress, and keeps them invested in the work. The check-in also provides built-in time to strengthen the relationship between the district lead and each FET principal.

Strategically, the annual conversation also prompts principals to clarify priorities for the next school year. While these check-ins feel informal and do not resemble an interview, there are a few beneficial talking points that can guide the conversations. You might start them by expressing genuine gratitude for principals' commitment and presence in FET gatherings. Take a few minutes to articulate and celebrate some of the team's main accomplishments. Then ask them a handful of questions, such as:

- How do you feel FET went this year?
- What are you most proud of?
- Do we need to discuss who will be leading the team next year?
- Looking back on the year, is there anything you wish that you would have done differently or that I could have done differently?
- Do you have any ideas on how you might be able to help the team share highlights of our efforts to the broader parent community and staff?
- What are your thoughts on recruiting additional staff for next year?
- How can I best support the team next year?

- What do you think are your school's areas for potential growth in terms of strengthening school-family partnerships?
- What are your best hopes for what the team might be able to address or accomplish next year?

These conversations can help the district lead develop a deeper understanding of what principals most value and what their hopes are for the FET team's future. When the district lead shares the highlights of each conversation with the team leaders toward the end of the school year, it plants seeds and offers direction to guide them during the following school year.

The annual reflection and visioning sessions with principals provide a valuable and needed opportunity for course corrections on the few teams that confronted unexpected challenges. For example, one FET team did a fantastic job of increasing parent participation and building a high level of camaraderie among members of the team. However, beyond the two teacher team leaders and the principal, they rarely had other staff attend. In addition, the team did not accomplish many tangible change efforts. In our conversation, the principal identified a few concrete ways that she would increase staff turnout the following year. She also said several times, "We need to get clear on what partnership with families means to us," and that she hoped moving forward the team would "identify strategies to strengthen relationships and communications between staff and families." These conversations can also lead to useful systemic insights as principals articulate ideas that often help both their team and every team across the district.

Create Synergy With Other School Improvement Efforts

FET action projects gain even more momentum when they are linked to related school improvement efforts that other entities have started. This is the case at every school level from elementary school to high school.

It is a common refrain to hear educators say that it is harder to engage the families of high school students. While the dynamics certainly shift, with students becoming more independent and teachers less likely to cross paths with families before, during, or after school, strong school-family partnerships are just as important and just as possible at the high school level (Mapp et al., 2022).

As Auerbach (2011) writes, "Parent involvement is known to decline during secondary school. But I am convinced that if you build it, they will come—as long as you create a supportive climate for parent activities and respond to parents' concerns" (p. 19). While a school can strengthen some aspects of their partnerships through efforts like FET, initiatives will ultimately be more effective if they are integrated into and prioritized within other structures and efforts at the school, no matter at what grade level.

Case Study: Centaurus High School

Centaurus High School's success in improving engagement with Latino families since launching a FET team in 2018 attests to the value of linking team efforts with other school improvement initiatives. At the four-year mark, their FET team had already established a high level of trust and accomplished a few important action projects. I asked the team leaders if there was a timely topic to explore that would intersect with other school efforts.

One of the team leaders pointed out that absenteeism seemed to be greater among the Latino student population. This seemed like the perfect topic to explore. Students not wanting to go to class speaks not just to attendance but also to engagement and ulti- mately themes that we had explored previously in FET meetings. We wanted to learn what data, if any, were available to shed light on this problem and what might be con- tributing to it. We asked the dean to present the data at a FET meeting. Then we would get parents' insights, hear from staff, and talk about what the group could do to turn the tide. We were a smaller group than usual—seven Latino parents, five educators including the assistant principal, a community leader, and the district lead.

"I want to be very honest," the dean began her short presentation of the data. "I see a certain disconnect between Latino students and our school. I want us to collaborate around how to develop more trusting relationships to support engagement and student success."

Latino students made up 27 percent of the total population, but when we looked at chronic absenteeism data (students with less than an 80 percent attendance rate), Latino students comprised 52 percent of that group. We had many questions planned to get the discussion started, but one in particular resonated with most of the group: What can we do as a school to improve the attendance of our Latino students?

One of the three fathers was the first to speak. "We need to look at how our Latino community was under attack in the United States for years," he said. "We were bullied persistently, and our kids feel that anxiety too. Who wants to come to school after that?"

The assistant principal was the next to share. He asked the team, "I recognize that these outside factors are playing a role, but what can we control as a school community?"

The one community leader in the room made a suggestion: "How about a survey of the Latino students? You could ask them why they are skipping class or don't feel as engaged."

A mother jumped in, saying, "Students are wondering what the point of school is. Mentally, emotionally, financially—families have gone through a lot of loss these last two years since the pandemic started."

This comment encouraged another mother to add, "Students need more emotional and social support, and to learn how to handle problems with others—conflict resolu- tion. I think we need students to have classes that are engaging like our FET meetings, on topics that matter to them."

The father who launched our conversation said, "I think that teachers need to do more meaningful activities to connect students with each other, for like five minutes at the beginning and end of class, and ask students for feedback."

One of the team leaders closed the conversation by echoing the spirit of FET in saying, "Without you, we can't figure all of this out. Let's keep this conversation going."

The sense of connection in the room was palpable, and many of us stayed around after the meeting closed. We had begun to collectively tackle two of the most challenging underlying issues the school was facing: low engagement and disproportionate absenteeism. Both families and educators shed light on potential next steps, and everyone left the meeting feeling better informed and more united around this shared challenge.

When the team met the following month, ten educators and sixteen parents were present. A team leader set the context for the discussion by revisiting some of the key attendance data and providing new data about the interrelationship between attendance and both grades and graduation rates. We learned that within the group of students with less than 80 percent attendance rates, nine out of ten students had at least one D or F. Figure 6.3 shows the graduation rate at Centaurus High School for various cohorts of students based on their attendance rates.

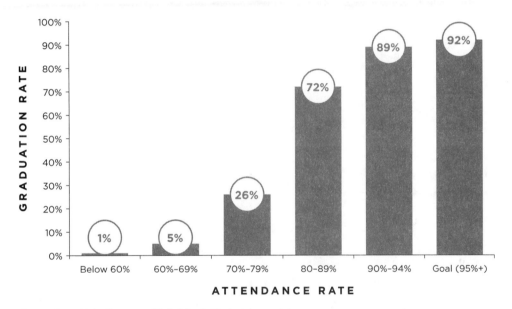

Source: © 2022 by Centaurus High School. Used with permission.

Figure 6.3: Centaurus High School graduation rate by attendance rate.

Team members divided into small groups of five or six people, and team leaders served as facilitators and interpreters in their groups as we discussed why students may be missing class and some solutions. This half hour was the most energized parents had ever been in the four years of the FET team. A number of insights were reached. For instance, team members felt that students might feel more welcome in class if teachers:

- Increased a feeling of belonging
- Led more interactive activities
- Discovered earlier in the year what students were most interested in
- Invited students to share more about their family and culture ("and not just in Spanish class!")

They also added that a more welcoming environment was possible if students felt treated equitably while also being seen as individuals, received more mental breaks and movement opportunities, and had a "peer buddy" to help them after an absence.

A week after our April gathering, the team leaders brought the parents' input to their multidepartmental multitiered system of supports (MTSS) meeting, and it informed that team's planning for next steps with both students and families. Soon after, they told me that their report sparked some of the best conversation at the MTSS meeting. The team leaders also conveyed that some colleagues became defensive upon hearing the parents' suggestions, but they encouraged them to analyze their feelings and take the feedback back to their department for some good discussion about how everyone can hold themselves accountable to make changes based on parents' input.

A few weeks later, when I met with the school's principal, he reminded me of what families had shared before we launched FET at Centaurus:

> When I arrived five years ago, we did not have the collaboration or communication with our Spanish-speaking families that we needed. It simply wasn't there. We now have a much stronger connection and partnership with all of our families, which ultimately helps us provide both opportunity and support to our students. (D. Ryan, personal communication, April 27, 2022)

Use Four Key Leadership Strategies for Effective Implementation

In the introduction (page 1), we examined in depth many of the obstacles to stronger relationships, trust, communication, and collaboration between schools and families. Whether you are a staff leader, parent leader, school leader, or district leader, you already know as a champion of partnership efforts that the road is not an easy or straight path.

Over these last two decades plus, as I have walked in your shoes, I've been humbled by the challenges and consistently aware of the windows of opportunity that we can seize or let slip away. Particularly from my vantage point as a district leader charged with supporting FET team leaders and principals to implement change, I have learned a lot about how to navigate the obstacles, work closely with colleagues to create small wins, and propel change—one conversation or action at a time.

By effectively drawing upon four strategies, you can greatly increase the likelihood that staff will invest in FET or other meaningful and impactful partnership efforts. Here are the key strategies for leaders to prioritize.

1. Why: Start with what matters
2. What: Get clear about your priorities
3. How: Tailor your approach to each of your allies
4. When: Build in the time

These leadership priorities should be continuously cultivated while implementing FET-initiated action projects and other tangible practices. Let's look at each of these vital strategies.

Why: Start With What Matters

While a school should not delay implementing new family-partnership practices until all staff are on board, effective leaders of change efforts should provide enough of the *why* before leaping to the *what* (Sinek, 2011). Before FET stakeholders introduce new family-partnership practices or reinvent existing ones, school leaders need to help staff members understand the benefits of changing their approaches to collaborating with families.

For instance, when I present about FET to a school staff after their principal has expressed interest in starting a team, I try to disrupt potential negative responses from some educators. These may sound like "We already know how to communicate and collaborate with family members," or otherwise convey a staff member's lack of awareness of how marginalized many underrepresented families at their school feel.

To convince them of the value of FET, I share quotes from families and educators at other schools (or ideally their own school) that speak to the need for FET, and contrast how families and educators engaged with each other before FET existed and after the team started. To also get at the *why* effectively, I share Anthony Bryk and colleagues' (2010) research, which shows that prioritizing and strengthening school-family partnerships is one of the five keys to shift from being a good school to a great school. Finally, I speak candidly about how my lack of awareness of this research led me to not focus on partnerships enough in my past work as a teacher and principal and the regrets that propel me to share this information widely.

What: Get Clear About Your Priorities

Steadily strengthening partnerships begins with intentionality on the part of FET principals and team leaders. I have had a long-standing appreciation for the Pareto principle, which says that 20 percent of our efforts lead to 80 percent of our outcomes (Kise & Holm, 2022). When I was a school principal, the dramatic improvement in school-family ties emerged primarily from two relatively small investments of time. We launched a positive phone call system that included the entire staff and led to a few hundred calls per year. The other impactful initiative was a monthly awards ceremony for students and families that consistently had a huge return on the time we invested as a staff.

During the first four years of my role leading the family partnerships department in my school district, I paid close attention to which initiatives had the biggest impact among the dozen-plus projects I was managing. In year four, when it became clear that the 25 percent of my role devoted to FET was reaping most of the benefits, I made an intentional and significant switch—I added six new teams to our roster of FET schools, and it became more than half of my role.

In doing so, I had to go through the challenging but needed process of ending several less-impactful initiatives. This shift was reminiscent of what I had learned as a principal about the importance of a "stop doing list," of things to deprioritize. I encourage you to reflect on some of the current partnership practices that you could discontinue or invest less effort in to free up time for more effective partnership efforts such as FET or other best practices that can be the focus of your team's FET action projects.

As your team identifies top priorities to strengthen school-family partnerships at your school or in your district, reflect on your one big thing or your top few initiatives. Here are four steps to help you get clearer on your priorities.

1. Make a list of all your existing efforts in the realm of communicating and interacting with families.

2. Reflect on your past experiences with these efforts (as well as what research on best practices indicates are the most high-leverage efforts).

3. Put a star next to the two or three practices that are likely to have the most significant impact on strengthening your ties with families and an X next to the efforts that you want to spend less time doing or stop altogether.

4. Create a SMART (strategic and specific, measurable, attainable, results oriented, and time bound) goal for each of your starred practices (Conzemius & O'Neill, 2005). For instance, if your list contains eleven practices related to your school's efforts with families, you might identify positive phone calls and home visits as your two high-leverage strategies and commit individually or as a staff to making three calls every Friday and two home visits on the first Monday of every month.

How: Tailor Your Approach to Each of Your Allies

As we have explored, most school staff are in a regular state of overwhelm, and consequently often view new initiatives negatively as "one more thing." Additionally, all but the most novice staff tend to be skeptical of new efforts due to years of witnessing their principal and district move from one reform to the next, often without giving adequate time to demonstrate the value of a new effort.

Knowing that this resistance is ingrained in most school cultures, we need to avoid persuasion or mandates, and instead capture educators' hearts and minds as we propose new FET-related efforts. In their book *Switch*, Chip Heath and Dan Heath (2010) show time and again that to effect transformative change, we need to reach both the rational mind and the emotional mind or, as they call it, the *rider* and the *elephant*.

For instance, when I introduced the positive phone call system during my final principalship, I used stories of actual students and families to reach educators' hearts. While this inspired their "elephant," many staff were rightfully concerned that it would be time consuming and interfere with other priorities. To reach their rational minds (their "rider"), I made sure to highlight the small time commitment that this effort would require. I also succinctly shared the research on the impact of positive communication with families.

Whether it is helping a FET school launch a positive call system or develop a cohort of staff members initiating home visits, I have found that the blend of data and insights from researchers alongside actual examples and testimonials from real practitioners is a powerful two-pronged approach.

When: Build in the Time

In my efforts to support schools with FET teams in efficiently and successfully implementing a school-family partnership best practice, one of the most consistent learnings has been the importance of the school leader building in time for staff to engage in these efforts. This is the most effective way to ensure that all staff experience and embrace a new strategy. As Eyal Bergman (2022) found in his in-depth study of successful partnership efforts, "teachers rate time regularly set aside for family engagement as the most helpful resource" (p. 22). Part of what makes FET so effective is that the time, as well as the structure and leadership responsibility, are built in. Rather than initiatives being stand-alone family partnership efforts and one person held responsible for carrying it out successfully, FET provides an ongoing vehicle for change accomplished through distributed leadership and propelled by diverse voices.

When leaders carve out time for staff, they are more likely to embrace partnership best practices. One of our high schools designates a morning before the first week of school to engage in neighborhood walks to visit students and families. At several of our schools, the principal designates fifteen minutes or more at the end of a faculty meeting for all staff to make a few positive calls to families.

When it is challenging to find the time but there is emerging interest among pockets of a school's staff, another effective approach is to compensate staff for giving their time. For instance, I have led several after-school home-visit training sessions, and paying educators for these couple hours is both an incentive and a way to honor their drive to become the champions or early adopters of this practice at their school. It also often leads these staff members to become more passionate about family-partnership practices and, among other benefits, join their school's FET team.

As I have discovered time and again with a diverse array of schools with FET teams, sometimes the best way for a partnerships practice to become successful is for it to grow organically. Instead of trying to get all staff engaging in the initiative at the same moment in time, a gradual approach can truly pay off. When the early adopters share with their colleagues how easy and rewarding they find a new practice, it piques the interest of other staff and often deepens buy-in because a peer has inspired them rather than having their boss expect them to take on this new effort.

Understand the Impacts of FET

Now that we have explored how to preserve the momentum of your FET team's efforts, let's look at some of the positive outcomes associated with FET teams.

FET Outcomes for Families

FET can help marginalized families feel that their voices are valued and essential to help the school address existing inequities. Team meetings affirm for parents that they bring needed expertise to help schools become more cohesive and just communities.

Families Feel Heard and Valued in Their Preferred Language

For many parents, a significant benefit of FET has been how important it is for them to have the opportunity to talk about their concerns in their preferred language. The FET environment feels safe enough for them to voice their concerns, knowing that they will be understood and supported.

In the report written after our first FET all-district parent leadership summit, many parents shared that FET is the only educational setting where they feel comfortable and secure enough to talk about difficult issues. Part of that comfort is based on the ability to speak their preferred language at meetings.

"There is now more communication between the teacher and us as parents," one mother at the summit said. "We feel free to express our thoughts about what we and our children need. We feel that we belong and that the school has us in mind. They take us into account."

A teacher leader added in her year-end reflection survey, "Parents made it very clear at our last meeting that they feel heard and seen and are touched by the lengths we go to plan fun, collaborative, informative, and listening-centered meetings where their voices and needs are the foundation."

Families Become Engaged Advocates

When parents learn the pathways for increased participation, they grow more determined to play an active role (Santana et al., 2016). Through conversations during FET gatherings or guest speaker presentations, families can gain access into the inner workings of the school *and* new insights into extending their learning at home. The team meetings help parents learn how to enhance their support of their child's learning.

As we have seen, FET buoys family members' capacity to meaningfully engage in their child's education. Schools—particularly ones that serve low-income, immigrant, and other marginalized communities—reduce inequities when they create ongoing opportunities to support parents' advocacy for their children's education (Santana et al., 2016). As a result of participating on the team, FET parents have often conveyed that they now talk with their children more about school.

The information discussed at FET meetings helps families navigate school with greater ease. For instance, at one FET meeting in an elementary school, a teacher provided a quick overview of the system used to help students resolve conflict. Families were also able to learn about the brain science that informs the practices their children use in class. This teacher's presentation at FET equipped families with greater knowledge of what happens in their child's classroom. It also provided them with the option to incorporate elements of this approach when helping their child resolve conflicts at home. Additionally, it supported their advocacy as they had time built into the meeting to provide the teacher with helpful feedback on the system. As one mother said, "FET is my lifeline toward the teachers and knowing that I can advocate for my son" (A. Avendaño Curiel, personal communication, May 12, 2022).

Families Form Stronger Bonds With Educators

I'll never forget what a high school student said as he shared his impromptu sentiments in the middle of a FET meeting at his former middle school. He had accompanied his father and younger brother to the gathering.

"When I was here," he said, "our (Latino) families didn't feel so comfortable. Now that we have these gatherings, we can trust the school more and not hide."

This theme of initially feeling marginalized but then of not needing to hide anymore has emerged at several FET schools. As a result of participating in FET, parents' confidence in engaging and communicating with staff significantly increases. The bonds that they forge with educators in the room typically transfer to trusting more of the school staff that their child works most closely with.

When I reflect on the teams that have built the strongest bonds between family members and educators, some of the primary factors behind their success in this area include the following.

- Educators proactively and regularly reach out to parents between team meetings.
- Teams are often led by a staff member and a parent, who model the kind of optimal rapport, trust, communication, and collaboration FET aims to build.
- Staff members on the team are intentional about conversing with parents during mealtime instead of choosing the more comfortable option of talking to colleagues. They also show more vulnerability by taking risks and being more authentic in their interactions.
- Team leaders demonstrate fidelity to the meeting structures that enhance the quality of connection between families and educators, such as engaging in dynamic team-builders, sitting in a circle with educators and family members interspersed, prompting team members to regularly connect through paired or small-group conversations, and having meaningful prompts in the introductory circle that help families and staff members discover both the similarities and rich differences that exist between them.
- Families and educators have opportunities outside of meetings to deepen relationships, such as home visits or optional gatherings outside of school like a parent-led cooking class or a staff-led hike.

Families Gain a Greater Sense of Community and Cultural Pride

In FET, family members also forge stronger ties with other parents. They begin to feel a greater sense of both community and collective power. Based on what parents from various schools have shared, I believe that they return to FET meetings as much to savor the deepening bonds with other families as they do for the meaningful dialogue or the connections they form with educators. Families experience this sense of kinship and solidarity that nearly everyone is longing for but is particularly important for underrepresented families. FET gives them a place to connect with their cultural roots.

At the final meeting of their first year as a team, Valicia, the parent leader at Eisenhower Elementary School, spoke to the cultural and communal importance of FET for her as a Latina mom. "It has been such a blessing to be part of this group," Valicia said. "I moved here several years ago. I came from a place where there was a large community of Latinos. I felt disconnected here. It feels like fresh air here being amongst my people" (V. Trowbridge, personal communication, May 7, 2022).

Families Become Agents for Change

FET also fosters greater parent leadership that galvanizes meaningful change. As one parent put it, "In my opinion the difference FET makes is that it helps us find solutions to the problems that are impacting our community. Many of us now look for opportunities that before we were just afraid to explore. As a result of the FET team, we have created a lot of change" (N. Argumedo, personal communication, May 12, 2022).

For example, in my district, three high schools collaborated to offer a Latino college night in Spanish, based upon parents' requests for more information about postgraduate opportunities in their preferred language. Another mother mentioned her passion for making art out of recycled materials at a team meeting and, shortly after, put up an altar in the school for the Mexican holiday Día de los Muertos (Day of the Dead). A few months later, she began teaching an after-school art class for students and families. A year later, she was asked to co-lead the FET team.

FET Outcomes for Students

It has been challenging to gauge how we would know the ways that FET was impacting the experiences of students whose parents participate on FET teams. In my district, we have never had the financial resources or bandwidth to launch large comparative studies of how "FET students" do compared to their peers whose families do not participate in FET.

Fortunately, parents and educators themselves have begun to naturally convey the very tangible benefits for their children. For instance, a mother at Eisenhower Elementary who had been shy and soft-spoken all year had this to share at the final meeting of their team's first year:

> From coming to FET, something happened with my kids. When I came the first time, they liked being here too. Afterward, they asked

me, "Mamá, when is the next meeting? Are you going to go?" It was motivating for me. Coming to FET helped my children a lot because they now are more confident and participate more in class, which they never did before. This happened because they saw me here and going to their meetings with the teacher. If they see me participating, they follow my example.

I was delighted to hear this testimonial that personalized and affirmed the research that when families partner more closely with staff, there are a host of positive outcomes for students (see figure 6.2, page 94).

Students Perform Better in School

In 2022, the Boulder Valley School District was the top-ranked district in the Denver metro area. Several schools participating in FET climbed in terms of their school performance ratings, moving from *improvement* to *performance*. Colorado has four school performance ratings, from lowest to highest: turnaround, priority improvement, improvement, and performance. The academic growth percentile of underrepresented students increased as well (R. Barber, personal communication, April 21, 2022).

When stronger school-family partnerships are in place, students experience a host of positive outcomes, including increased motivation, higher grades and test scores, a greater sense of self-efficacy, and deeper levels of class engagement (Mapp et al., 2022). Across the diverse array of schools that have FET, we have seen that when families and educators are on the same team, students seem to feel more supported, empowered, accountable, and inspired to bring forth their best.

Students Improve Relationships With Family and School

Parent participation in FET not only supports students' cultural pride and academic engagement and growth, but it also fosters or deepens their connection to their school and leads them to see their school as a source of strength.

Natasha Gupta, a mother of Indian descent, shared the following sentiment about the impact that her and her husband's participation in FET has had for her son. "He has been struggling with other children making fun of the food he brings from our home," she said. "When he sees us here at FET with families from many parts of the world, it shows that every culture is valued and that his differences are something to be proud of" (N. Gupta, personal communication, April 4, 2023).

Louisville Middle School and Fireside, the neighboring elementary school, were both heavily impacted in the middle of their teams' first year by the most destructive wildfire in Colorado history, which destroyed nearly one thousand homes. I will never forget sitting in a circle with parents and staff at our FET gathering at the Fireside Elementary, three months after the fire, and a mother sharing with us, "My child feels so connected to the school that when we were driving back into town, in the middle of the massive fire, she was singing the school anthem as a sense of security."

FET Outcomes for Educators and Schools

FET benefits teachers and school leaders in countless ways. It deepens educators' respect and understanding of families and builds their capacity to skillfully partner with them. They also discover the joy and meaning that comes with a more human connection to families and relationships rooted in deeper trust.

"FET has given me the gift of deeper connections and being able to communicate with families," one middle school teacher shared in a meeting. "I think that's what education should be—a partnership that you see all angles of. It's very beautiful and transformative."

Educators Learn More About Students and Families

FET leads educators to develop insights on how to serve students and families alike more effectively. This happens largely because educators can better understand parents' perspectives, strengths, and challenges after hearing their voices in FET, in ways that rarely emerge in parent-teacher conferences or other educational forums. Educators who participate in FET bring their new insights as well as their inquiries back into the classroom to ultimately benefit students.

Participating in the team is also one of the best ways for educators to strengthen their cultural competency, which is fundamental for improving communication and building stronger relationships. It also translates to stronger learning outcomes. For instance, one study revealed that teacher awareness of the culture and community of their students led to a 10-percentage-point increase in reading scores and a remarkable 24-percentage-point increase in mathematics scores (Marschall, 2006). FET teams are building a bridge between educators and families and a school community that includes them both.

Educators Become More Satisfied With Their Jobs

Research shows that this deeper commitment to partnering with families leads educators to report high levels of job satisfaction and greater interest in remaining in the profession (Hong, 2019). Staff members feel more connected to and loyal to their students' families because they have built such strong bonds with them, and vice versa. When educators and family members work together in partnership, they both change their beliefs and expectations of their counterparts (Mapp et al., 2022). Equally important, educators become more aware of how they can contribute to stronger partnerships, and their sense of agency significantly increases.

Additionally, FET leads educators to shift away from the conventional belief that families must change for relationships and collaboration to improve. Instead, they realize that they hold the bulk of the responsibility when a partnership initiative is faltering, which can lead school staff to take more ownership around needed changes.

Through their participation on the team, family members and educators grow steadily more confident and vocal in pursuing needed changes. In essence, they each acknowledge their interdependence and use it to inspire shared action. Their collaboration creates tangible change and disperses the responsibility for creating a just school.

Schools Can Better Meet Educator, Student, and Family Needs

Beyond the many testimonials from families who have participated in FET that speak to its importance for them and for their schools, we possess quantitative data that indicate its impact for schools and their most prized stakeholders: students, families, and educators.

When we surveyed parents from across the dozen-plus FET schools at our first FET Parent Summit, we asked them to evaluate several statements and compare how they would rate them before FET existed and now that their school has a FET team. The Likert scale we used was:

1. Not at all true (poor)

2. A little bit true (not too good)

3. Somewhat true (OK)

4. Quite true (good)

5. Definitely true (very good)

Of the seventeen items on which they shared their input, table 6.1 shows the averages for the items that matter most. The difference in scoring before FET existed and the current valuation speaks to the concrete ways that FET has steadily transformed their experience with their child's school, their perspective on educators, and the level to which they feel valued and seen.

Table 6.1: Parent FET Survey Results

Survey Item	Score Before FET	Score After FET
There is a good relationship between teachers and parents.	3.0	4.3
Educators treat parents with respect.	3.6	4.7
There is genuine collaboration between school and parents.	2.3	4.3
The administration wants all students to be successful.	3.0	4.6
My culture and my values are recognized and supported.	3.1	4.4
The staff at my child's school value my opinion.	2.9	4.7
Teachers show respect toward students.	3.4	4.5
I trust the staff at my child's school.	3.0	4.5
My child is doing well academically in school.	3.4	4.8
I feel connected to my child's school community.	2.8	4.7
My child feels part of the school community.	3.2	4.5

These results, and the shift that FET propelled, are based on the power of collaboration between families and educators.

Additionally, as public schools grapple with declining enrollment and related budgetary strains, building a welcoming school community where all stakeholders feel a strong sense of belonging leads families to keep their children enrolled and attracts new families. My colleague John McCluskey shared the following reflection about the impact of FET in his first four years as principal at Centennial Middle School:

> As a result of this improved sense of community, due largely to FET, we have doubled the enrollment of our emerging bilinguals in the last four years from 19 percent to 39 percent. I am convinced that FET has played a pivotal role. As families have seen and felt the genuine desire for us to engage them thoughtfully, like all of our parents, they tell their friends that we are a place where their students will feel safe and be able to progress as learners. (J. McCluskey, personal communication, January 27, 2022)

As the number of teams has grown over the years, we have built a strong network (or *FETwork*) across many of our schools, which helps the entire system steadily transform. When all FET leaders gather quarterly, successful change projects at one school circulate and have possible ripple effects for other schools. When leaders share their insights and action steps with others, it expands other teams' awareness of both the remaining barriers within the system and the practices to propel schools toward a more promising future.

Conclusion

In FET, the path to great outcomes comes not from an unwavering orientation toward tasks and goals, but from putting people and process first. By doing so, we create the fertile ground for self-sustaining teams that create lasting changes.

Building or deepening partnerships between educators and families is a vital and underutilized pathway for creating the kinds of schools that all our children deserve. Through our efforts in FET to implement best practices to transform school culture, we elevate voices that urgently need to be heard. In doing so, we are building bridges to a more promising future for all students, families, and educators.

Questions for Reflection and Discussion

1. Which action projects did you find most compelling, and why?
2. After reading this chapter, what new insights do you have about the most significant barriers in your school or district and potential next steps?

3. Of all the outcomes mentioned for families participating in FET, which feel most timely for or needed by the families that you work with?

4. Reflecting on the benefits for educators that we explored in chapter 1 (page 19) and the outcomes from this chapter, which ones do you think would best make the case to your colleagues about committing to deepening partnerships?

5. If you had two minutes to convey to colleagues the value of forming a FET team, what would you say?

Epilogue

Traveler, there is no path.
The path is made by walking.

—Antonio Machado

As I was in the middle of writing this book, my wife gave birth to our first baby. I was aware of the deep attachment between caregiver and child after spending two years as a foster parent some years ago. Nonetheless, I have been in constant awe of the immense love that I feel for our daughter, who is on her playmat beside me as I write these words. There is something special about the bond we build when we are with them from their first day and sacrifice sleep and so much more to ensure that they thrive.

My experience, like that of countless parents, sheds light on the untapped potential for stronger school-family partnerships. Every parent feels deeply invested in the current and future well-being of their children. As a result, we are inclined to do what we can to ensure that their time at school maximizes their growth.

If as educators we look at every family as a potentially outstanding ally rather than an occasional interloper, we can better harness the power of partnerships. Additionally, if we enhance our approach—both in the practices we use and the spirit in which we engage in them—we can overcome existing obstacles, improve collaboration, and strengthen our ties.

A few days before I began writing this epilogue, a dear colleague and friend sent me a compelling email. He informed me that he had rediscovered a few passages about school-family dynamics that my mother, Rachael Kessler, had written in her book, *The Soul of Education*. He provided me with the page numbers and nothing more.

Encountering the following words reminded me of both the challenge and opportunity that invite us to elevate our existing efforts:

> As a teacher, I was surprised how easy it was to fall into an "us versus them" mentality with parents. As educators, we have often separated ourselves from parents out of fear that they would criticize us for not being good enough for their "darlings." Then, as a parent, when

> my own children entered high school, I was surprised at how easily
> I felt intimidated by teachers who would judge me for not being a
> good enough parent or who held so much power over the future of
> my child. (Kessler, 2000, p. 164)

My mother went on to share that when educators and families come together on behalf of supporting children's growth, "they also help strengthen the adult community essential for soulful approaches to survive in schools. . . . Working together, teachers and parents become, if only for an evening or a semester, a team of elders collaborating to raise the next generation" (Kessler, 2000, pp. 165–166).

Based on my two decades in schools and troves of research, I think it is fair to say that educators are consistently in a state of overwhelm and often reluctant to take on more. FET provides a vehicle for family-partnership initiatives not to launch in isolation but instead to be woven into the fabric of the school's operating system. It ensures that efforts are "integrated and elevated" (D. Hutchins, personal communication, October 15, 2021), collaboratively driven, and ultimately successful.

Any system created by humans can be transformed by humans as well (Robinson, 2009). If we are going to effectively create more just and collaborative educational systems, we need to make key decisions together. More important, perhaps, we need to change the ways in which we approach our partnerships—both the *how* and *why* that drive our work with families.

I'll close with one final story. In 2022, I attended a FET meeting at Boulder High School, where I had graduated twenty-seven years earlier. We had just reached the closing minutes of the gathering. The six parents and six staff members were visibly tired, but the sense of mutual appreciation was palpable. After a rich and lengthy conversation, it was too late for us to do a closing activity, so we asked if anyone had any final reflections.

"I am realizing the importance of communication," said the school counselor. "It is obvious that it's important and it helps our families as well as our students. But it often falls through the cracks as we get swept up in every challenge that surfaces on any given day. As a staff, we have to deepen our commitment to communication."

Her words reflected the exact kind of realizations that FET is intended to lead educators toward. Before we wrapped up, I was hoping that we would hear closing reflections from a parent too. That voice quickly surfaced.

"I just want to say that I am so grateful to have a FET team here," a mother said. "I have had children in this district for fifteen years. For those of us who have been at schools without FET, we know what it can be like. Without FET, we [underrepresented families] often feel like we have no voice, no opinion, no value. When my daughter graduated from middle school and I had to say goodbye to that FET team, I was so relieved to know there was a FET team here. I knew that we would be valued and that our children would be seen as important."

What would our schools be like if we had more of these types of encounters? As we explored in the introduction, there continues to be a host of barriers to creating stronger partnerships within our education system. Due to this emphasis on breadth over depth, educators often feel fragmented and default to maintaining the status quo in order to survive. As a result, trust levels remain low as families experience most interactions with educators as transactional rather than relational.

The barriers we have explored are not immutable. We need to break down the walls between educators and families as well as the ones between educators themselves. The ruptures can be repaired, and stronger bonds can be developed. Many of us are hungry for these changes and know that, as Audre Lorde put it, "Without community, there is no liberation" (as cited in Birdsong, 2020, p. vii).

We also need to let go of outdated ways of engaging with families. Instead, we can embrace high-leverage practices that strengthen our ties, increase trust, propel learning, and are not time intensive. Throughout this book, we have seen that greater synergy and positive changes are possible when we prioritize relationships and use a clear structure for harnessing ongoing collaboration.

The Families and Educators Together model is just one piece of the puzzle in reimagining and transforming our school communities. FET's dual priorities of being human centered and change oriented make it an excellent compass for change in this era of greater isolation, overwhelm, and divisiveness.

This partnership between families and schools may appear to be a small, peripheral program that impacts primarily underrepresented families. But from my perspective, it is far more than that. It is an efficient, meaningful, and proven pathway to transform a school community from the inside out.

When we as educators create a place where families of diverse backgrounds can thrive, it makes our schools safer and more effective for all students. It shows that, no matter who you are, what language you speak, or what your skin color may be, our schools care about you. This goes far beyond closing the achievement gap. It is about opening our hearts to each other and making our communities stronger and more welcoming to stakeholders of different backgrounds and perspectives.

I hope the human beings and teams you've learned about in this book will inspire you to take bold steps. If we deepen our commitment to fortifying relationships and cultivating meaningful school-family partnerships, the arc of public education can be forever changed. By building bridges across differences and innovating around our shared interests, we pave the way to a better future for everyone.

APPENDIX A

Frequently Asked Questions

Appendix A is a detailed list of frequently asked questions that can help you as you plan your FET meetings.

How do you respond when there is low attendance at FET meetings?

There can be months where only a few parents attend the team meeting, particularly in a team's first year. Try to avoid this predicament by consistently using all the recruitment and ongoing communication strategies highlighted throughout the book. If you have a month with underwhelming parent attendance, take a few minutes in the planning session with the district lead and team leaders to explore potential root causes, and also consider broader, more relational reasons. Ask questions, such as "Do families still lack strong ties with anyone on the staff?" "Did we not offer enough information about what FET is or the particular focus of the meeting in our communication?" For the next meeting, develop a more robust outreach plan.

For example, you might ask the principal to send texts or make calls to families so they're more motivated to attend. Or choose a timely topic for family learning time or invite an appealing guest speaker. For instance, when Eisenhower Elementary struggled with parent attendance in their second year, the team leaders and I determined that inviting district officials to discuss school safety would get parents in the door, and attendance increased from four parents the previous month to fifteen the month of the school safety exchange. Over time, we've also learned how effective it is to add a hook to the communication, such as "we need your input as our school begins searching for a new principal" or "a special raffle will be held." You can also send thank-you messages to the parents who attended the last meeting and engage in more personalized or in-person outreach to parents who have been regulars but were absent from the most recent meeting.

When there is low attendance at the start of FET meetings, do you begin on time?

It is not uncommon for some teams to have several parents arrive late. How many family members will attend can be a source of anxiety and suspense. While some parents will politely say *yes* when they receive the invitation phone call, you will never know exactly how many parents will be in attendance. Part of the rationale of starting with dinner is that the more structured portion of the meeting does not begin until the fifteen-minute mark, so there is time built in for late arrivals.

If there are at least two parents present at the end of mealtime, go ahead and begin the meeting. In the rare instances where no parents have arrived or only one, you may want to discuss related topics but not start the agenda until more parents have arrived or you reach the half-hour mark. I have participated in several gatherings where we had a rich and meaningful conversation with just two parents in attendance. While that number is disappointing, it always provides the opportunity for a more intimate learning session and exchange between staff and families.

In what circumstances are FET gatherings postponed or canceled?

We have occasionally postponed or canceled a meeting when there is a crisis or a safety concern at a school that same day. However, sometimes in those circumstances we still hold the gathering, as it creates a helpful space for both families and educators to process the day's events.

You will likely choose to postpone when weather conditions are dangerous or school has been closed. In fact, as I write this, our district today had its first snow day of the school year. One team decided to postpone, and the other team shifted to holding the gathering virtually.

How do you encourage families that are shy or deferential to participate and make suggestions?

As we explored in chapter 4 (page 59), families can be reluctant to make constructive comments or suggest new ways that the school could partner with families, particularly in the initial team gatherings. When a new team was on the verge of launching, a principal shared with me, "Many families tell me that the school is great and they wouldn't change anything when I ask them how we might improve. I'm concerned that families will shy away from making comments that may help us learn and do better for them."

While I had a few approaches to share with him that had worked well at other schools, I wanted to confirm these were effective with a parent leader before assuming I knew the right answers. The very next day, I was in a planning meeting with Kanako

Nishimura, a team leader, where we discussed how to include families from multiple Asian countries. Kanako's insights paralleled what I had seen work well:

> Many of us come from collectivist countries where people value harmony more than anything else. To keep harmony in our societies, we have been told to be loyal to authorities. Suggesting new ideas for improvement or rejecting ideas from people with authority, such as teachers or principals, is considered disrespectful in some Asian countries. Also, many people from these countries prefer not to stand out too much to keep harmony in a group. Considering their background and values, the best thing that a team leader can do to support families to overcome this is to invite someone to make a comment and then immediately praise them for doing so. That will encourage all the other families to see that different perspectives and suggestions are not just welcome but also very much appreciated. (K. Nishimura, personal communication, January 23, 2023)

What is *open forum* time, and how often does it happen?

As we explored in chapter 4 (page 59), FET meetings have a reliable and consistent structure. Parents' comments and input at one meeting often shape major portions of the agenda at the next meeting. However, the team leaders and district lead do determine the content of each aspect of the agenda. As a result, there can be tremendous value in building in space for *open forum*, which essentially is time for families to bring up what is most important for them to share or discuss in that moment.

A question you might ask to get open forum started is, "What is something that you'd like to share that would be helpful for us to know?" or "Based on what has been going on lately for your child or for your family in terms of connecting with the school, what is on your mind that you'd like to share?"

At one team's meeting, we came into the evening with an agenda focused on questions for families, but families were eager to talk about safety in the wake of a threat called into the school earlier that week. This ultimately led to a great conversation around how the school could improve its communication in times of crisis. At another school, we were ready to focus our time on next steps with the team's FAQ project, but parents wanted to talk about mental health supports for students at a particularly difficult time in the school year.

Over time, we have learned the value of incorporating open forum time into our agendas as often as possible. While there is always the risk that one or two parents may hijack the focus of the meeting, it is absolutely vital to create opportunities to ask families what matters most to them and not allow the agenda to be driven solely by the priorities of the team leaders.

How do you build a sense of continuity between meetings? Do you know when you leave a meeting what the next gathering's focus will be?

Part of what makes planning FET meetings such a dynamic and creatively rewarding process is that you don't usually have a clear sense coming out of a meeting what should happen at the next one. It is usually quick and easy to pull a new team-builder from the bank of options and generate a prompt for the opening circle that relates to that time of the year or will help everyone learn something about the personal life of each participant. For the family learning time portion of the meeting, you may have a prioritized list scheduled a few months out or quickly determine the optimal guest speaker based on comments and needs parents have expressed.

However, it can often be challenging to determine what themes or questions should comprise the meaningful dialogue portion of the next meeting, particularly if there was a sense of completion on a topic at the previous gathering or the team has recently accomplished an action project and it is unclear what the next area of focus should be.

Here is a concrete example of how two team leaders and I turned this challenge into an opportunity to create a strong new agenda. These unanticipated plans emerged organically from our conversation. We realized that the final round of parent-teacher conferences would take place two weeks after the next meeting, so we incorporated a small amount of time for families to review a list of questions that they could ask teachers during these upcoming conversations.

Two meetings prior, families had learned how to navigate the student portal called Infinite Campus and learned other technology tips as well. We decided that the second part of our dialogue time would be checking in to ask them how using these tools had been going. It then dawned on us that there was a professional development session the week prior to conferences where we could incorporate time for each staff member to text updates to select families on their child's academic progress. This would address the gap in communication that parents had commented on the previous school year. Questions for parents would include, "What do you want communication to look like in these academic updates? Should teachers highlight missing assignments, behaviors, or grades?" When I asked one of the team leaders what a sample text might sound like, she said, "Your child is at the approaching level."

I then asked, "Will they know what that means, or is standards-based grading likely something that they are unfamiliar with?" This led us to integrate a ten-minute portion where this team leader would explain standards-based grading to families and leave time for their questions. Finally, since the previous meeting had a guest speaker on mental health, but there had not been sufficient time for families to engage in dialogue, the FET team would resume the mental health conversation. As you can see, reflecting on past meetings and prioritizing what might be both most relevant for families and most insightful for staff propelled the creation of this agenda.

What are some of the topics that schools have explored in family learning time?

Family learning time feels particularly important at the middle and high school level, as FET teams strive to fill information gaps that have accumulated for parents since the start of their time in the school system. For this portion of FET meetings, which is typically around fifteen minutes but can occasionally last as long as thirty minutes, topics for families have included the following:

- How to use the apps designed for families to check their students' attendance, grades, and assignments, and communicate with staff
- Strategies to help children more effectively deal with stress or conflict
- The school counselor explaining their role and the school's Positive Behavioral Intervention and Supports (PBIS) system
- Information on scholarships and how to apply for college and financial aid
- The ways that mathematics is taught differently today compared to when family members attended school
- An overview of what bullying is and how it differs from other student-to-student conflicts

If nonimmigrant White parents want to support a FET team, how can they contribute?

If a White parent feels passionate about the purpose of FET, they can work behind the scenes to help recruit staff and underrepresented families to join the team. A few White parents have played a key role in a school deciding to launch a FET team. White parents of a biracial or multiracial child are included in FET meetings if they are interested in attending.

As we make changes to the partnership practices at the school, White parents can also serve as additional voices that encourage the school leaders and staff to make these positive changes. On occasion, a White parent who leads the PTA or another organization may ask to join a FET team meeting to better understand what FET is and to build a reciprocal relationship between FET and the parent organization that they represent. The structure of a FET meeting could also work effectively for a gathering of educators and families of any racial or cultural background.

What are some tips for district leads to effectively coach FET team leaders?

As I learned from my nine years as a school leader, district leads build rapport and gain trust faster and more effectively by not offering constructive suggestions in the first months of collaborating with team leaders. For instance, my first year of coaching team leaders involved quietly observing, prioritizing relationship building with them, attending all planning sessions, offering precise praise, and making subtle suggestions as the leaders and I reflected on what went well and what could be improved.

While I was cautious about "taking over" during the facilitation of team gatherings, I was aware from my days as a basketball coach and an instructional leader that one of the best ways to provide guidance is through modeling. I began to lead activities that allowed team leaders to see how certain facilitation moves positively impacted the group.

As renowned doctor Atul Gawande puts it, "Coaching done well may be the most effective intervention designed for human performance" (as cited in Knight, 2022, p. 3).

What is one of the more interesting questions or topics that has surfaced in a FET meeting?

We can always learn from other countries how to improve our ways of doing schooling. At several FET meetings, we have asked teams that are comprised primarily or entirely of parents who went to school in other countries, "What is something you appreciated about your own school that is missing here at your child's school?"

Parents' comments have been fascinating and insightful. For instance, one mother said, "In Israel, we have informal SEL after school that helps students and families connect with one another, and it is often led by parents." A mother from Thailand talked about how meditation was incorporated for fifteen minutes a day in her classroom, which led the teacher leader to comment that the school should integrate mindfulness practices more often into the classroom. A parent from Japan talked about how students clean their own classroom daily, which fosters a sense of responsibility and unity. A mother who had been a teacher in China talked about how meaningful it was for parents to be able to visit the classroom and shadow their child for a portion of the day, which led the principal at that school to turn that idea into a next step.

APPENDIX B

Organizational Tools

Appendix B includes a sample districtwide FET calendar, a rubric for understanding family partnerships, and a year-at-a-glance FET timeline.

Sample Districtwide FET Calendar

The sample districtwide FET calendar from Boulder Valley School District featured in figure B.1 (page 128) can help you ensure there is minimal or no overlap between FET meetings at different schools. Since there are numerous schools and meetings listed on the calendar, I have found that it helps to visually differentiate between planning sessions and actual FET meetings. As such, I always highlight the planning sessions in a different shade, as shown in the calendar.

	MONDAY	**TUESDAY**
First Week of the Month	Fireside Elementary School; 5:00–6:30 p.m.	Mesa Elementary School planning; 4:00–5:00 p.m. Centennial Middle School; 6:00–7:15 p.m. Louisville Middle School; 6:00–7:30 p.m.
Second Week of the Month	Louisville Middle School planning; 10:25–11:10 a.m. Fireside Elementary School planning; 11:45 a.m.–12:45 p.m. Lafayette Elementary School; 5:30–7:00 p.m.	Eisenhower Elementary School planning; 12:20–1:20 p.m. Centennial Middle School planning; 4:00–5:00 p.m. Boulder High School; 6:00–7:30 p.m.
Third Week of the Month	Angevine Middle School planning; 11:20 a.m.–12:20 p.m. Lafayette Elementary School planning; 3:00–4:00 p.m.	Boulder High School planning; 5:30–6:30 p.m.
Fourth Week of the Month		Columbine Elementary School planning; 10:45–11:45 a.m. Crest View Elementary School planning; 2:00–3:00 p.m. Pioneer Elementary School planning; 3:30–4:30 p.m. Manhattan Middle School; 6:00–7:30 p.m. Mesa Elementary School; 6:00–7:30 p.m.

Figure B.1: Sample districtwide FET calendar.

WEDNESDAY	THURSDAY	FRIDAY
New Vista High School planning; 9:00–10:00 a.m. Whittier Elementary School; 4:00–5:30 p.m. Eisenhower Elementary School; 6:00–7:15 p.m.	Angevine Middle School; 6:00–7:30 p.m.	
Louisville Elementary School; 5:30–7:00 p.m. Crest View Elementary School; 6:00–7:15 p.m.	Centaurus High School; 5:30–6:45 p.m.	
Manhattan Middle School planning; 8:15–9:15 a.m. Centaurus High School planning; 9:45–10:45 a.m. Whittier Elementary School planning; 3:00–4:00 p.m. Fairview High School; 6:00–7:30 p.m.	Pioneer Elementary School; 5:00–6:30 p.m. Columbine Elementary School; 5:00–6:30 p.m. New Vista High School; 5:30–7:00 p.m.	

Moving Toward Authentic Family Partnership Rubric

This reproducible rubric is a synthesis of research, particularly Susan Auerbach's (2011, 2012) work on authentic school-family partnerships. It is organized around the four pillars for partnerships that I devised for Boulder Valley School District in 2018: (1) two-way communication, (2) relationships and trust, (3) learning and well-being, and (4) decision making and power. I created the rubric in 2018 with colleagues at the University of Colorado Boulder as a tool for schools to self-assess their current state and have a more concrete pathway to making progress along the continuum. It can be useful to draw upon this rubric when launching your FET team as a tool for analyzing where your school would like to focus its initial partnership efforts.

Moving Toward Authentic Family Partnership

	Undeveloped Family Partnership	Developing Family Partnership	Traditional Family Partnership	Authentic Family Partnership
Two-Way Communication				
Two-way and reciprocal	• Communication for most families is limited to informing them of major shifts in school programs and structures or emergencies.	• Almost all communication goes from school to home. • There are limited times and ways for families to communicate with the school.	• Families give input in some contexts, such as on committees, through surveys, at parent-teacher conferences, or with key staff.	• Families communicate with the school in multiple ways. • School staff and families listen to each other in multiple settings.
Consistent and accessible	• Communication is sporadic and not always translated to languages other than English spoken in the community, or is not translated well and in accessible language.	• Communication is somewhat regular with some translated materials, but families must make an effort to access information, especially in languages other than English.	• Communication is consistent through key methods (such as newsletters, weekly folders, email, key school staff), with important (but not all) communication translated and understandable.	• Communication with families occurs on a consistent basis in understandable language. • Communication occurs through a variety of methods based on families' preferences (such as phone calls, texts, auto dialers, in person, email, and social media).
Relationships and Trust				
Welcoming and affirming community spaces	• Families do not feel welcome in the school building. • The front office may feel intimidating or unfriendly.	• Families feel welcome in some spaces, such as specific classrooms, but not others.	• Families feel welcome in multiple places in the school. • The school reflects multiple cultures and many staff are bilingual, friendly, and helpful.	• There are spaces in the school for families to access or contribute to resources. • There are spaces for marginalized families to take on leadership roles. • The school acts as a resource for families, in partnership with community organizations.

page 1 of 4

	Undeveloped Family Partnership	Developing Family Partnership	Traditional Family Partnership	Authentic Family Partnership
Authentic care	• Educators make little effort to learn family members' names and other information about the students' families.	• There is a perception that formally educated parents are more involved in their children's education.	• Families give input on particular decisions and in traditional settings (such as school committees, surveys, and parent-teacher conferences).	• School staff and families get to know each other in multiple ways (such as home visits, community dialogues, caring everyday interactions, opportunities for listening at school events, and so on).
Strengths-based views	• Families are talked about as a "bother." • There are common stereotypes about marginalized families (such as, they don't value education or have time to contribute).	• School staff and highly visible family members try to accommodate marginalized families' needs but are not aware of their needs or practices firsthand.	• Marginalized families are included but may be primarily sharing language skills, food, or cultural practices.	• Families' various strengths and interests are recognized, valued, and welcomed as part of the school community.
Intercultural understanding	• It is expected that marginalized families should learn and adopt the school's practices.	• Cultural practices are added to existing events or practices (such as a song at a concert, building displays, food at events, marginalized families invited to join existing committees, and so on).	• There are events aimed at bringing families together to learn about a variety of cultural practices (such as Diversity Night or Diversity Week).	• School practices and events are co-created by school community members and include a variety of cultural practices; community members develop intercultural understanding.
Trust	• Educators and families barely know each other. • Families may fear retribution for speaking up.	• Educators work closely with a selective group of family members who contribute to the school.	• A community or family liaison or other key staff members are connected to marginalized families, but trust tends to be limited to just a few key people.	• Most or all teachers and staff have trusting relationships with a wide variety of family members, including marginalized families.

Learning and Well-Being

Supporting student and family learning	• Families must ask for information if they want it. • Parent-teacher conferences focus on sharing students' scores or grades and behavior without inviting families to share what they know about their children.	• Communication about learning largely occurs through grading systems (such as Infinite Campus) and short parent-teacher conferences, with minimal translation available. • Families must wait a considerable amount of time to speak to teachers for a few minutes at conferences.	• Communication about student learning occurs through back-to-school nights, parent-teacher conferences, and phone calls home or meetings with families when there is a celebration or concern. • The school provides events and resources to help families understand the school's systems and support student learning at home.	• Families learn from the school or partner community organizations about how to support their children's learning. • School staff are aware of how families support their children's development. • Connections with families integrate student learning and value children's whole academic, social-emotional, and moral development.
Supporting student and family well-being	• School staff are focused only on academic achievement. • Attending to social-emotional well-being is not the role of the school.	• Resources are available for emergency services and care. • Packaged parenting workshops are offered (such as "Love and Logic").	• There is a social-emotional learning focus in the school, possibly through a curriculum or program, which families are informed about. • There are groups of families who care for one another.	• The school provides resources, spaces, and events to support students' and families' social-emotional well-being. • Community members know and care for one another.

Decision Making and Power

Participation in decision making	• Families are seen as unnecessary to the school functioning. • Educators do not have time to work with families.	• Families are seen as resources who contribute through volunteering, fundraising, and adopting the school's practices. • Visible family members coordinate family contributions.	• Families have a say in their children's learning. • Visible family members participate on school committees. • Decision-making opportunities may be limited to small decisions or driven by school leaders.	• Decision-making settings (such as committees) are made up of members representing the whole school community. • Educators and families make decisions together about the school's programs and practices.

On the Same Team © 2024 Solution Tree Press • SolutionTree.com
Visit **go.SolutionTree.com/diversityandequity** to download this free reproducible.

	Undeveloped Family Partnership	Developing Family Partnership	Traditional Family Partnership	Authentic Family Partnership
Sharing power	• There is little attention to differences in power. • School leaders make decisions and inform staff and families as needed.	• Families have limited opportunities for input, such as surveys. • There is little to no attention paid to ensuring that participation reflects the diversity of the school's population.	• Marginalized families have key advocates (such as liaisons or visible family members) that give input on school decision making. • Decisions are largely made by school leaders, with input from staff and some family members.	• Traditionally marginalized families' input is essential to school decision making. • Educators' and families' knowledge, expertise, and perspectives are included and equally valued. • There may be spaces or groups specifically for marginalized families.
FET team functioning	• There is a lack of school leadership support. • Decision making is controlled by team leaders or school leaders. • There is a lack of representation of families and educators on the team.	• There is sporadic support from school leadership, or the school leader controls the decision making. • Team members give some input into decisions but the outcomes are largely determined by team leaders or strong team members. • There is some representation of marginalized families on the team, but their participation is limited.	• School leadership is consistently present. • The team shares in decision making, but there are some strong team members who tend to dominate discussion and action.	• The team has strong, but not controlling, support from school leadership. • Team members reflect the diverse array of underrepresented families within the school community. • Teams privilege the participation of families who are often underrepresented on school committees (including the language used in meetings and all voices being elevated and heard). • Team members' contributions are equally valued.

FET Year-at-a-Glance Timeline

This timeline can help you align your FET planning with the school calendar.

▸ AUGUST

- New FET leaders meet for a two-hour training.
- Team leaders identify their team meeting day and time after checking the school calendar and confirming that FET teams at neighboring schools are not meeting on the same evening.
- Team leaders identify their monthly planning date and time in collaboration with the district lead.
- District lead creates the FET districtwide calendar.
- Team leaders and district lead secure childcare and interpretation support for the first meeting and ideally beyond.
- Team leaders and school leaders determine which staff will regularly attend team gatherings.
- District lead shares FET shared drive and list of to-dos for team leaders prior to first FET gathering.

▸ SEPTEMBER

- Team leaders and district lead hold first planning meeting two weeks or more prior to the first team meeting.
- FET team holds its first meeting.
- District lead transfers budget to each team.
- Families are recruited through multipronged outreach efforts.
- First quarterly all–team-leaders meeting is held at the end of the month.

▸ OCTOBER

- Teams brainstorm family learning topics for the remainder of the school year.

▸ NOVEMBER

- Team leaders, principal, and district lead confer in brief discussion around team goals and how principals can support with implementation of goals.
- Second quarterly all–team-leaders meeting is held at the end of the month.

▸ DECEMBER

- Teams clarify their action projects for the school year and share with district lead.

▸ JANUARY

- District lead provides annual FET update to district leadership.

page 1 of 2

▸ FEBRUARY

- Team leaders develop clarity on how the team will complete all change projects in and between the February, March, and April gatherings.
- Third quarterly all-team-leaders meeting is held at the end of the month.

▸ MARCH

- Teams place existing roster and other key documents in district FET shared drive.
- District lead clarifies which schools will add new teams next school year.
- Any FET leaders not continuing into the new school year notify the district lead.

▸ APRIL

- New FET leaders are selected and engage in an onboarding conversation.
- District lead and principals hold annual FET reflection and visioning conversation.
- District lead presents FET overview to staff at prospective new schools.
- District lead determines budget for the next school year.
- Teams conclude action projects or develop a clear timeline for implementation if project is geared toward the following school year.

▸ MAY

- Final team gatherings are held at least ten days before the final day of the school year.
- Final planning session takes place between district lead and team leaders at every school to share principal's reflections and input, and capture any useful FET ideas for next year.
- FET Parent Leadership Summit for all schools is held three weeks or more before the end of the school year.
- Final quarterly all-team-leaders meeting is held a few weeks before the end of the school year.

APPENDIX C
Outreach Materials

Appendix C includes samples of outreach materials and a reproducible information sheet that you can use to share the word about FET with others and aid in recruitment.

Sample Information Sheet for Families

Figure C.1 is an example of an information sheet about FET that you might share with families.

Join Our FET Team!

What Is Families and Educators Together (FET)?

FET is a team of family members and educators partnering together for the success and well-being of all students. FET aims to center the voices of families whose experiences are traditionally underrepresented and collaborate with educators to see how we can improve the school for the benefit of all.

Why Participate?

Children do their best when parents and teachers are a team. Everyone's voice is needed and helps us create a stronger school community for all. We want to hear what *you* think would make our school a better, more inviting, more equitable place. You will also make connections with other families, strengthen ties with staff, and learn more about the inner workings of our school.

When?

One meeting each month, plus whatever extra help you want to provide! Our monthly meetings are held in person at school from 5:00 to 6:30 p.m., with childcare, dinner, and interpretation provided.

What Do Participants Say?

"FET means building community and staying engaged with the school." —FET parent

"FET makes me feel more safe when I need to communicate with the school staff. I feel supported and trust them." —FET parent

"Here we are family. It is not us and them; it is us together." —FET teacher

"FET supports our community and makes us feel that we belong and the school has us in mind." —FET parent

"FET brings us together to get to know each other better. It also helps us find solutions to the problems and gaps that are impacting our community." —FET parent

Who Do I Contact?
Parent Leader: Amanda Morales (XXX) XXX-XXXX; AmanMorales@XX.com
Teacher Leader: Laurie Boyer (XXX) XXX-XXXX; LBoyer5@XX.com

Figure C.1: Sample information sheet to share with families.

Sample Flyer

Figure C.2 is an example of a flyer that you might use to engage the school community.

Figure C.2: Sample FET meeting flyer.

Sample Messages From District Lead to Team Leaders

The following four sample emails can inspire communications with team leaders.

Email to Team Leaders, Prior to Start of School Year

To

Subject

Dear FET leaders,

Welcome back! I hope you each had a great summer. New team leaders—it was wonderful seeing all of you on Monday, and thank you for joining us.

To make it easier for you and your team leaders to successfully get FET in motion this year, I've put together the attached checklist (attach a copy of the checklist shown in figure 3.1, page 52) that you can use as a guide over the next several weeks. The calendaring tasks at the beginning of the document are the only timely part of the list that I'd appreciate you taking care of by next Friday. The rest of the guide you can attend to as time permits.

As always, I'm available if you have any questions or if I can be of help in any way.

I look forward to connecting with you later this month to help you plan your first meeting. In the meantime, thank you for taking on this rewarding leadership opportunity and have a great start to the new school year!

Ari

Email to Team Leaders, One Week Into the School Year

To

Subject

Dear FET leaders,

I hope you each had a wonderful first week of the school year. While it's hard to say goodbye to summer, it is great to see all the positive energy around the start of this new school year.

A few quick updates and reminders: I am working on a couple of different fronts to help you line up childcare for your FET meetings. I'd like to set up a system to make securing childcare easier and more reliable. I met with a local group that is interested in helping us, but need to know soon which day each FET team is holding their monthly meeting.

Here's what I need from you today or tomorrow to get them what they need. Please reply to this email (to me and copying your team leaders, not Reply All) with your school name and a *yes* or *no* to having childcare, such as "Crest View FET meeting will need childcare."

Last, if you haven't done so already, please add your FET meeting date to the all-teams FET calendar. I cannot move forward with identifying childcare support from our providers until I send them the calendar with the dates for every team. Thanks to all of you who have done so already! I'll reach out individually to those of you who haven't identified your planning time with me yet, so we can have that time built into our calendars for the rest of the school year.

I'm excited to support each of you as you get things in motion for a great first FET gathering at your school.

Ari

Email to Team Leaders, Two Weeks Into the School Year

To

Subject

Dear FET leaders,

Good morning! I hope you each had a great weekend. Here are a few helpful resources for your leadership of FET that I've been eager to share with you for a couple months. They are also in the shared drive.

1. First is a call script that you can draw upon and make your own (attach a copy of the family call script on page 144).

2. The second resource includes team-building activities for the opening of FET meetings (attach a copy of the team-building activities on page 151).

3. The final resource gives suggested small-group talk structures (attach a copy of the resource on page 148).

Please take a look at them at your convenience any time this week, and let me know if you have any questions.

Ari

Email to Team Leaders, Three Months Into the School Year

To

Subject

Dear FET team leaders,

I hope you are all doing well as the holiday season nears. Here are just a few updates and reminders as we continue to build great momentum with our FET efforts. Many of you know that I prefer to send one detailed and timely message every so often rather than several emails, so please read this at your convenience sometime this week.

Thank you for your ongoing dedication to building stronger connections with families via FET. I know how much hard work you put into each gathering and the demands of a night meeting after a full day of work, and deeply appreciate your leadership! The fruits of your efforts are evident both in the strong attendance (even in our first snow storm earlier this month, one of our new teams, Angevine, had their highest parent attendance yet) and in the levels of comfort and trust parents are showing through the candor of their comments.

Our next quarterly FET team leaders' meeting is right around the corner, on the Tuesday we return from Thanksgiving Break. As I requested at this time last year, I'll be giving each school some time to capture in a few sentences the top two or three emerging priorities that your team has identified to focus on as action projects for change. This will help you crystallize your focus so that you can accomplish these goals in the second half of the year. It also gives us the opportunity to share succinctly with upper district leadership all the outstanding changes you are creating within your school communities when I have an annual FET update with them in January. In anticipation of our team leaders' meeting on November 29, **please be thinking about and ready to capture that afternoon your team's main existing or emerging action steps,** and consult with your principal as needed to continue building momentum on these goals.

As we have learned from previous years, if we are clear by the end of our December FET meetings what our change projects are, there is enough time in the second half of the year to accomplish those projects while continuing to achieve other aims during our team meetings.

Finally, as many of you know, last May we held our first FET Parent Leadership Summit, with participating families from across our FET teams. I'm attaching the detailed report here for those of you interested in reading or scanning it during a quiet time in the weeks ahead. It contains many powerful comments and insights from our families and some compelling data about how FET has changed their experience at your school and ideas to move our work forward.

I savor the time collaborating with each of you and feel so excited about what is unfolding through our FET efforts at seventeen of our schools (with an eighteenth and nineteenth school joining us in January). Thank you for your continued dedication to FET amid so many competing priorities. As I shared with folks from other districts last week, **the research tells us that developing stronger school-family partnerships is one of the five keys to turning a good school into a great one,** yet it often is overlooked, is done in a one-way fashion, or falls low on the staff's priority list. Thanks to your leadership in FET and the great support of your principals, you are prioritizing partnerships and ensuring your school becomes a more inclusive and connected community for everyone.

I look forward to seeing everyone for our next FET leaders' gathering on the November 29. For those that I won't see this week, I hope you can savor time with your families and friends, and that you have a wonderful Thanksgiving Break!

Ari

Sample Messages From Team Leader to Families

The following examples can inspire communications with families.

Sample Start-of-Year Outreach Email for Families

To

Subject

Hello Fireside Families!

Please join us at our first FET team meeting of the year on Monday, September 19, 5:00–6:30 p.m., near the intermediate playground. Childcare will be provided, and we will enjoy a dinner together at the start of the meeting. If this time is difficult for your family, you are welcome to arrive late or leave early. Any participation is appreciated! Interpretation will be provided, if needed. Spanish interpreters will attend each meeting, and if you would like an interpreter for a different language, please let me know and we can make arrangements.

You are receiving this invitation because we would love for you to be part of FET at Fireside this year! The previous school year was Fireside's first year of FET, and we hope to expand our team this year. Our goal as a FET team is to make cross-cultural connections, learn about diverse perspectives, and find ways to support and celebrate each other, as well as improve our school and the Fireside community. Please view our FET recruitment video to learn more about FET at Fireside. You can also visit our FET website for more information or to view the agendas or community notes from our meetings.

This invitation is being sent to all English language development families, as well as other families at Fireside who represent diverse groups. Please extend this invitation to other diverse families you know at Fireside, or you can send me their names and I will reach out to them. Our invitation includes all forms of diversity.

I will continue to send FET team communications to everyone on this list, unless you let me know that you would rather not receive these communications. I understand we all have very busy lives and flooded email inboxes, and will not be offended if you decline our invitation or communication. If there is another email or an additional family member you would like me to add to this list, please let me know.

Sincerely,

Shelby Warshaw

Source: © 2022 by Shelby Warshaw. Used with permission.

Family Call Script With FET Talking Points

Hello, my name is _____ and I am a _____ [role here] at _____ [school name here]. I am a member of FET, which is a team made up of families and educators who work together to create a better school community for all. FET is also a space to get to know other families from underrepresented populations and collaborate with the staff.

We would like to invite you to our first (or next) FET meeting. The meeting is _____ [day of the week and date] in _____ [location and school name]. We will have dinner and childcare available. We want to hear your voice and benefit from your input. We know that listening to what families think helps us create a better, more welcoming, and more equitable school. Are you able to join us?

Talking Points for Phone Calls or Flyers

What is Families and Educators Together (FET)? FET is a team where you can:

- Express your ideas on how to make your school an even better place for your children
- Share ideas and learn from other parents
- Meet and collaborate with teachers and your principal
- Connect with other (Spanish-speaking or multilingual) parents
- Learn more about your child's education

We want to hear your voice and benefit from your support.

Overview of FET to Share With Stakeholders

Families and Educators Together

Our district is dedicated to building collaborative relationships between schools, families, and the community to support the achievement, success, and well-being of every child. Families and Educators Together (FET) teams provide a structure to prioritize and enhance school-based family partnership activities, particularly with underrepresented families.

Participating schools will create FET teams strategically focusing on the school's family partnership work. Each participating school will receive a stipend to support the work of its FET team, for both the team leaders and the team itself.

What Is a FET Team?

A FET team consists of educators, administrators, parents, and community members who meet monthly to develop a plan for school, family, and community partnerships. The team collaborates for the success and well-being of all students. Family members bring forth their voices to discuss with staff how to build a more inviting, equitable, and overall stronger school community for all.

We Already Do Family Partnership Work. How Is a FET Team Different?

Over fifty years of research shows that not all family partnership practices are equally effective in impacting overall student success (Epstein & Associates, 2018). At the same time, families and school staff alike can feel stretched by the many family involvement activities and initiatives they are requested to invest time and energy into over the course of the school year. Having a FET team allows schools to prioritize and focus the school's family partnership initiatives to ensure that they are directly supporting school improvement goals and that they are achieving the intended impact. A FET team also propels schools to enhance their existing approach to four key pillars at the heart of our partnership efforts:

1. Engaging in two-way communication
2. Cultivating relationships and trust
3. Supporting learning and social-emotional well-being
4. Sharing decision making and power

What Will Happen to the Family Partnership Activities That We Already Do?

Having a FET team does not mean that schools have to scrap the family partnership activities that they already do; it is merely a framework to look at all of the school's family partnership activities and analyze how they fit into an integrated family partnership strategy that supports the school's goals.

Who Is on the FET Team?

A FET team typically has at least ten members and includes:

- Between two and five team leaders (teachers and parents or guardians)
- The school principal
- Three or four teachers from different grade levels (If the school has an English language department program or MTSS leadership team, it is recommended that a teacher from each of those programs is part of the team.)
- Four to six parents or guardians from underrepresented communities (At least half the team should be family members who are not school staff.)
- A community liaison (if your school has one)

page 1 of 2

The FET team could also include:

- Community members, including business partners, volunteers, interfaith leaders, and representatives from literary, cultural, civic, and other organizations
- Students from different grade levels (for high school FET teams)
- Other stakeholders who are central to the school's work with families, including the school nurse, social worker, instructional aide, counselor, other administrators, front office staff, custodian, or others

What Is the Time Commitment for FET Team Members?

Team Members

- Attend monthly FET team meetings (typically ninety minutes long)
- Commit to help with FET events and activities
- Commit to an estimated two hours per month for meetings, subcommittee meetings, and events

Team Leaders

- Commit to an estimated three to five hours per month for meetings, subcommittee meetings, events, preparation and communication with team members, and meetings and communication with the district representative
- Attend a new leaders' training as well as FET leaders' gatherings, held four times a year, to support their leadership
- Collaborate monthly for an hour with the district lead to begin planning the next FET meeting

What Are the Benefits of Having a FET Team?

- Family partnership activities are prioritized so that staff and parents do not feel stretched and can focus and work together on what is most important for student success.
- Underrepresented families feel heard, and their insights benefit the staff's learning.
- Families feel supported and have opportunities to learn about resources and structures that empower them to support their child's well-being and educational journey more deeply.

What Are the Next Steps to Get Started?

- Have a conversation with the district leader to discuss whether FET is a good fit for your school.
- Optional: if it seems like FET would be a good fit for your school, the district lead can come to one of your faculty meetings to do a brief presentation on the FET framework. Faculty will decide whether they want the school to participate.
- The district representative will work with the principal to identify leaders for the FET team. An initial overview training will be scheduled at the beginning of the school year for FET team leaders.
- The district representative will work with the principal and team leaders to identify FET team members.

References

Epstein, J. L., & Associates. (2018). *School, family, and community partnerships: Your handbook for action* (4th ed.). Thousand Oaks, CA: Corwin.

APPENDIX D
Meeting Activities

Use the following lists of dialogue structures, team-building activities, and discussion questions to help plan your FET meetings.

Dialogue Structures

Calling Conditions

This is a great activity to do at the closing of a gathering. It helps develop reflection skills and deepens the sense of community in a group. Team members stand in a circle. The facilitator asks everyone to check in with what they are feeling at the moment and gives them a minute of silence to think. After the moment of silence, the facilitator says to the team, "Let's each call out one word or phrase that expresses one of the things we're feeling right now." If two people overlap, the facilitator slows the responses down and lets each person repeat their word. This activity can also be done moving clockwise in an established order. This dialogue structure was created by colleagues at the Passageworks Institute.

Chalk Talk and Gallery Walk

The facilitator poses questions or topics that participants write down at various stations around the room. Participants move between stations, writing their thoughts. At the end, each person walks around the gallery reading everyone else's writing.

Consensus Circles

The facilitator puts participants in small groups of four to eight people and poses a question. Participants write their thoughts in response to the question on a note card. A volunteer starts the sharing circle by reading what they wrote on their card. The sharing continues clockwise, and participants have the right to pass. The facilitator can also build in time for dialogue at the end of each round.

Fist to Five

The facilitator reads the statement or proposed decision that the group needs to come to consensus on. Participants indicate their position by using their fist or fingers to indicate their degree of agreement:

> No fingers (fist): "No, I can't live with that decision"
> One finger: "Not convinced; let's talk more"
> Two fingers: "Could go along with it"
> Three fingers: "OK"
> Four fingers: "High on my list"
> Five fingers: "All for it"

The leader scans the hands and reflects the data back to the group or uses the data in the decision-making process.

Huddles

Participants quietly walk around the room for a few moments (there could be background music, but silence is fine too). The facilitator then has team members form standing huddles by saying, "Huddles of three" or "Find two other elbows (or shoulders) to connect with." The facilitator poses a question or topic for all huddles to discuss and lets everyone know the total amount of time they will have to share with each other. When the allotted time concludes, the facilitator encourages participants to thank their huddle mates and then walk around the room again until they're prompted to form another huddle with people who were not with them in the preceding one. Mixing up the size of huddles as the group engages in a few rounds of this process makes the activity more dynamic, and gives each participant the opportunity to talk with a variety of people over a relatively short amount of time.

Jigsaw

The facilitator places participants in several small groups where they will discuss a unique topic with their group members. Assign a number to each small group. After providing time for discussion and any note-taking, form a new group that contains as many participants as there were groups; for example, if there were five small groups, each new team should have five members. The members of these new groups should all have been in different groups originally, as they will be sharing what their first group discussed. Provide a set amount of time for each person to serve as an "expert" by sharing the highlights of the discussion they had within their original group.

Inside-Outside Circle or Wheel Within a Wheel

Participants form two circles, one inner circle that is then ringed by an outer circle. Participants then engage in a timed pair share, with the facilitator indicating whether the participants on the inside or outside of the circle speak first. Whichever participant is not speaking should be actively listening and does not give a verbal response. The facilitator then asks participants in either the inside or outside circle to rotate a specific number of spots clockwise, and engage in another timed pair share with their new partner. The facilitator calls a number, and the person with that number from each team shares their response.

Numbered Heads Together

The group is divided into teams. Participants number off. The facilitator poses a problem that needs to be discussed and provides the participants think time. Participants privately write their answers, then stand up and "put their heads together" in groups, discussing their answers. The facilitator calls a number, and the team with that number shares their responses.

Sentence Completion

In small groups, participants engage in several rounds of sharing based on a given prompt, such as "One of the things that I most appreciate about our school is _____." After all participants have contributed, the facilitator provides a new sentence starter, and the activity continues.

Snowball

Each participant writes their name on a piece of paper and records information about themselves before wadding up the paper. This can be any information, or something specific prompted by the facilitator. Participants form either a circle or two equal lines, each half on either side of the room. At a signal from the facilitator, they begin a snowball fight with their crumpled paper. When the facilitator calls time, each team member reads their new (or thrown by another member) snowball, learning new information about the person whose snowball they found, and then shares it with the group (Gibbs, 2006).

Stand Up, Hand Up, Pair Up

The facilitator begins by saying, "When I say 'go,' stand up, put your hand up, and pair up!" After a pause, the facilitator says, "Go!" Participants stand up and keep one hand high in the air until they find a partner. The newly formed pair high-five each other and then put their hands down. The facilitator asks a question or gives a topic for discussion and partners engage in a pair share (Kagan & Kagan, 2009).

Timed Think-Pair-Share

The facilitator announces a topic, announces how long each participant will have for sharing, and then provides think time. After the think time, participants form pairs. The first partner shares their response to the prompt while the second partner listens. The second partner responds with an affirmation. Partners then switch roles (Kagan & Kagan, 2009).

World Café

Team members gather at tables in small groups within the meeting space. Each table will have a host who stays at the same table throughout the activity and ensures everyone gets a chance to speak. There will be two to three rounds, each with a different question that the group addresses. During the rounds, all participants can take notes or draw images that reflect the major points of conversation. After the first round, everyone but the hosts will mingle and move to another table. Before beginning the second and third rounds, the hosts will give a one-minute summary of the table's conversation on a piece of chart paper in the middle of the table from the previous round.

References

Gibbs, J. (2006). *Tribes learning communities*. Windsor, CA: CenterSource Systems.

Kagan, S., & Kagan, M. (2009). *Kagan cooperative learning*. San Clemente, CA: Authors.

Team-Building Activities

3-2-1

Participants pair up and face their partner. The facilitator calls out a series of numbers, 1, 2, and 3. For each number, participants should do the following:

- When the facilitator calls "1," participants do a right-hand high five with their partner.
- When the facilitator calls "2," participants do a left-hand high five with their partner.
- When the facilitator calls "3," participants high-five with both hands.

The facilitator calls out a series of the numbers ("1, 2, 3"), and partners must do the correct clap sequence. The facilitator continues calling various series of three numbers ("2, 1, 3," "3, 1, 2," "3, 3, 1"). The activity becomes more challenging with a four-, five-, or six-number sequence ("2, 2, 3, 1" or "1, 3, 1, 2, 3").

Bumpety-Bump-Bump

Participants stand and form a circle, with one person in the center. The "center person" (who is *it*) walks up to someone, stands in front of them, and says one of the following:

- "Center, bumpety-bump-bump"
- "Self, bumpety-bump-bump"
- "Right, bumpety-bump-bump"
- "Left, bumpety-bump-bump"

The person receiving the command must say the name of the person who is *it* for "Center," their own name for "Self," or the person's name to the right or left of them before the person who is *it* completes saying "bumpety-bump-bump"; otherwise they become the next *it* (Gibbs, 2006).

Gotcha

Team members stand in a circle, arm's-length apart. The facilitator asks participants to extend their right hand out to their side, palm up, and with their left arm to hover their left index finger roughly six inches above the extended palm of the person on their left. On the count of three (or, often more effectively, using a thematic word like "watermelon" or "rabbit"), participants have two aims: to catch the hovering index finger of the person on their right with their right hand and avoid having their index finger caught by the person on their left.

After two rounds, participants switch sides so that their left palm is facing upward and their right index finger is extended; this helps wake up the other side of each person's brain. (If the facilitator is using "go" words instead of counting, they should say other thematic words before the "go" word—for instance, if the go word is "watermelon," the facilitator may say, "Pineapple, raspberry, peach, watermelon!"). This activity was created by colleagues at the Passageworks Institute.

Group Juggling

Standing in a circle, participants begin with their hands out in front of them, ready to catch a ball. The facilitator begins the activity by saying one person's name and throwing the ball to this participant. Participants then toss the ball person to person in a repeat pattern around the circle, with everyone getting the ball only once. Once the pattern is established, the goal is to maintain the pattern, tossing the ball more smoothly from person to person and dropping the ball as little as possible.

page 1 of 4

Depending on how much time teams have to play and how quickly the group picks up the game, they may increase the difficulty by adding one or two balls to be tossed in the same pattern. At this point, participants' awareness of the other balls becomes important so that balls do not collide in the middle of the circle. This activity was created by colleagues at the Passageworks Institute.

Put Yourself on the Line

The facilitator asks the group to stand up. The facilitator then describes an imaginary line down the center of the room, which will act as a continuum. The facilitator identifies the two positions at either end of the line as "strongly agree" and "strongly disagree," and indicates that the middle position is for those who have no opinion, choose to pass, or are "moderates." The facilitator tells the participants to move to places on the line that express their feelings or opinions on statements that the facilitator calls out—for example, "Schools should be the main community hub for families" (Gibbs, 2006).

Rainstorm

The facilitator has everyone sit or stand in a circle, facing the center. They then ask all participants to close their eyes and pause for a moment or two for the room to become quiet. Each person gets ready to hear the sound the person on their right will be making. The facilitator tells participants to keep their eyes closed as the rainstorm begins. The facilitator or a selected participant starts the rainstorm by rubbing their palms together, back and forth. The person to the left joins in, and then the person to their left joins, and so on, around the circle.

When the person who started the rainstorm hears the drizzle sound of rubbing palms being made by the final person, the first person changes from rubbing their palms together to snapping their fingers. When the snapping action has been picked up by everyone around the circle, the first person switches to hand clapping, then to thigh slapping, and finally to foot stomping. After foot stopping, the order of sounds is reversed, proceeding from thigh slapping to hand clapping, then to finger snapping and finally palm rubbing. This activity was created by colleagues at the Passageworks Institute.

Rhythmic Clapping

Participants stand in a circle. The facilitator says, "I will turn to my right, and _____ will face me. We will look each other in the eyes and then at the same moment, clap our hands. Then _____ will whirl around to their other neighbor and look them in the eye and at the same moment clap hands." This activity is continued around the circle, and then the group tries to repeat the sequence with a graceful rhythm.

As the team nears completion of the first round, the facilitator can tell the group that they are going to repeat it another round in the same direction, or the facilitator may have participants reverse direction. As a final round, the facilitator encourages the group to go faster and faster until it's going as fast as it can go. When the facilitator feels the activity is finished, they encourage the group to gift itself with applause. This activity was created by colleagues at the Passageworks Institute.

Snap, Clap, Stomp

The facilitator has participants break into pairs, one partner facing the other. Their task is to count to three again and again, as fast as they can, alternating numbers. Partner A says "One," partner B says "Two," and partner A finishes the triplet by saying "Three." As soon as they've finished, they start again, this time with partner B leading by saying "One," so the counting loops around in continuous fashion. After a minute or so, the facilitator checks in with players to see how it went. People who have done this activity are often surprised by how difficult it proved to be.

After that first round, the facilitator offers directions for the second. With the same partners as before, players count back and forth again, but instead of saying "One," participants should snap, not clap. Now, the sequence starts with a snap, before partner B says "Two" and then partner A says "Three.

For the third round, instead of saying "Two," players now clap so the rhythm goes clap, snap, "Three." Otherwise the activity is the same—same partners, alternating back and forth, going as quickly as possible.

For the fourth and final round, the entire pattern becomes kinesthetic, with "Three" being replaced by stomping a foot. The activity has now shifted all the way from saying "One, Two, Three" to all physical movement: snap, clap, stomp. At this point, the activity becomes like a step routine, a rhythm to sink into.

Spider Web

This activity starts with a sturdy ball of yarn. The facilitator holds the end of the yarn in one hand and unravels the ball of yarn enough to be able to toss it across the circle to another person. Before throwing the ball of yarn, the facilitator, keeping hold of the end of the yarn, says the name of the person they are throwing it to, then tosses the yarn and asks them a question, such as "What kind of music do you like?" Then the person who has caught the ball of yarn answers the question and, while holding onto a length of the yarn, tosses the ball to the next person, says that person's name, and asks a question.

This continues until everyone in the room is holding part of the unwound ball of yarn, which will form a kind of web. (The facilitator should make sure that people throw the yarn across the circle. The game does not work well if people toss the yarn to the person next to them or even two over from them.) The last person to receive the yarn will toss it back to the facilitator, as the game begins and ends with the facilitator. This activity was created by colleagues at the Passageworks Institute.

Step In

Participants stand in a well-spaced-out circle. The facilitator asks a question or makes a statement. Participants to whom the statement applies "step in" by taking one large step into the center of the circle. Participants to whom it does not apply remain in their original spot in the circle. The facilitator makes another statement, and the process repeats itself.

Some sample statements include the following.

- Step in if your family has four members.
- Step in if your family likes to swim.
- Step in if your family has a grandparent living in your house.

This activity was created by colleagues at the Passageworks Institute.

Two Truths and a Lie

This activity is ideal for small groups, but can be used with a larger group. Participants write three statements about their life, such as major accomplishments or hobbies. Two of these statements should be true, but one should be made up. The first participant begins by reading their statements. Teammates announce their guesses or can hold up one, two, or three fingers to indicate their guess. The person who made the statements reveals which is false. This continues with each group member.

What Are You Doing?

In a circle, one participant mimes a familiar action (such as brushing teeth). The partner asks, "What are you doing?" The performer states another action that has nothing to do with what they are doing (such as riding a bicycle). Now the "asker" must perform the action (in this case, riding a bicycle). The partner asks, "What are you doing?" and the other names another action; the asker then performs that action, and so on. This can also be done as a group, with one person performing and the group responding. This activity was created by colleagues at the Passageworks Institute.

The Wild Wind Blows

Participants arrange chairs in a circle, with one fewer chair than there are players. Everyone sits, except for one leftover person, who stands in the center. The person in the center says something that might be true for some or all participants, such as "The wild wind blows for those who like the mountains," or "The wild wind blows for those who love Thai food." Everyone for whom that statement is true scrambles to find another chair, including the person who is standing in the center. The person remaining without a chair has the next turn in the center. This activity was created by colleagues at the Passageworks Institute.

Zen Counting

The facilitator instructs the group members to count aloud individually from one to ten, starting with whoever wants to start. Participants must watch each other carefully. Taking turns, each participant says only one number. No other words are to be spoken. If one participant talks over someone else or repeats another, the exercise starts back at number one.

References

Gibbs, J. (2006). *Tribes learning communities*. Windsor, CA: CenterSource Systems.

Questions to Ask in FET Meetings

Questions for Family Members
- What are you most proud of about your child?
- What are your hopes and dreams for their experience at our school?
- What experiences have you had with schools in the past?
- What do you value that prompted you to attend this meeting? What commitment are you willing to make to the success of the effort?
- What do you want to contribute, and what do you want to learn about?
- What do you want to know about us?
- What are you hearing from your child about how school is going? What would you like us to know?

Questions for Paired or Small-Group Trust-Building Conversations

Universal Questions
- What is your favorite family activity?
- What would your ideal job be?
- What is a piece of wisdom you have learned from a relative?
- What is your favorite birthday meal?
- If you could travel to any country in the world, where would you go, and why?
- What is your idea of perfect happiness?
- What is your greatest fear?
- Which historical figure do you most identify with?
- Which living person do you most admire?
- What is your greatest extravagance?
- On what occasions do you think it's OK to lie?
- Which words or phrases do you most overuse?
- When and where were you happiest?
- Which talent would you most like to have?
- If you could change one thing about yourself, what would it be?
- If you could change one thing about your family, what would it be?
- What do you consider your greatest achievement?
- What is one of your most treasured possessions?
- Where would you like to live?
- What do you most value in your friends?
- If your friends only had three words to describe you, which three do you think they would use?
- Since our last gathering, what has happened in your life that you would like others to know about?

School-Centered Questions
- What does your child tell you about school, or what sense do you get of how they feel about school? (To ask staff: What do you think your students highlight in what they share with families?)
- In what ways are you feeling supported by your child's teacher and the school's staff? What else would be helpful? (To ask staff: What do you think families most appreciate?)

page 1 of 2

- What are some ways that you have felt connected to and included in our school community? Are there other examples of how you have felt disconnected or excluded?
- How can we create a school culture of greater acceptance and belonging?
- Do you feel like you belong in the community? Why or why not?

More Questions for Parents From Peter Senge's (2000) Schools That Learn

- What strengths do you see in your child?
- What does your child say about school?
- What kinds of activities, at school or elsewhere, seem to frustrate your child most?
- What kinds of activities excite your child? What do they play?
- Tell me about your child's peers and social relations? Who do they socialize with outside of school?
- What kinds of responsibilities does your child have at home?
- What goals do you have for your child?
- What goals does your child have?
- What is your child's favorite subject or activity?
- What would you like me to know about your child? (pp. 224–225)

References

Senge, P. (2000). *Schools that learn: A fifth discipline fieldbook for educators, parents and everyone who cares about education*. New York: Knopf.

REFERENCES AND RESOURCES

Achor, S. (2018). *The happiness advantage: How a positive brain fuels success in work and life*. New York: Currency.

Adams, K. S., & Christenson, S. L. (2000). Trust and the family-school relationship: Examination of parent-teacher differences in elementary and secondary grades. *Journal of School Psychology*, *38*(5), 477–497.

Arrien, A . (2001). The way of the teacher: Principles of deep engagement. In L. Lantieri (Ed.), *Schools with spirit: Nurturing the inner lives of students and teachers* (pp. 148–157). Boston: Beacon Press.

Arundel, K. (2022, August 5). *Survey: Majority of parents say schools' customer service needs improvement*. K–12 Dive. Accessed at www.k12dive.com/news/majority-of-parents-say-schools -customer-service-could-improve/628932 on August 5, 2022.

Auerbach, S. (2011). Learning from Latino families. *Educational Leadership*, *68*(1), 16–21.

Auerbach, S. (2012). Conceptualizing leadership for authentic partnerships: A continuum to inspire practice. In S. Auerbach (Ed.), *School leadership for authentic family and community partnerships: Research perspectives for transforming practice* (pp. 29–51). New York: Routledge.

Barton, A., Ershadi, M., & Winthrop, R. (2021) *Understanding the connection between family-school engagement and education system transformation: A review of concepts and evidence*. Accessed at www.brookings.edu/wp-content/uploads/2021/10/Understanding_the_Connection_FINAL .pdf on August 21, 2022.

Benigni, M. D., Haeffner, B. A., & Lehman, L. B. (2022). *The great equalizer: Six strategies to make public education work in America*. Lanham, MD: Rowman & Littlefield.

Bergman, E. (2022). *Unlocking the "how": Designing family engagement strategies that lead to school success*. Learning Heroes. Accessed at https://bealearninghero.org/unlocking-toolkit on August 17, 2022.

Birdsong, M. (2020). *How we show up: Reclaiming family, friendship, and community*. New York: Hachette.

Boulder Valley School District. (2020, July 31). *Excellence through equity in BVSD* [Video file]. Accessed at www.youtube.com/watch?v=iGw0tDWW21Q&feature=youtu.be on August 21, 2022.

Brooks, D. (2023, February 16). America should be in the middle of a schools revolution. *The New York Times*. Accessed at www.nytimes.com/2023/02/16/opinion/america-schools-revolution.html on July 27, 2023.

Brown, B. (2015). *Daring greatly: How the courage to be vulnerable transforms the way we live, love, parent, and lead*. New York: Penguin.

Bryk, A. S., & Schneider, B. (2004). *Trust in schools: A core resource for improvement*. New York: Sage Foundation.

Bryk, A. S., Sebring, P. B., Allensworth, E., Luppescu, S., & Easton, J. Q. (2010). *Organizing schools for improvement: Lessons from Chicago*. Chicago: University of Chicago Press.

Budge, K. M., & Parrett, W. H. (2022, September). Mapping the family-engagement continuum. *Educational Leadership*, *80*(1), 10.

Cadogan, M. M. (2022, September 29). Keeping families of color connected. *Educational Leadership*, *80*(1), 84–86.

Campbell Jones, B., Keeny, S., & Campbell Jones, F. (2020). *Culture, class, and race: Constructive conversations that unite and energize your school and community*. Alexandria, VA: ASCD.

Cashman, L., Sabates, R., & Alcott, B. (2021). Parental involvement in low-achieving children's learning: The role of household wealth in rural India. *International Journal of Educational Research*, *105*(4).

Chapman, B., & Belkin, D. (2022, September 1). Fourth-grade test scores plummet. *The Wall Street Journal*, p. A3.

Chappuis, J. (2005). Helping students understand assessment. *Educational Leadership*, *63*(3), 39–43.

Cisneros, S. (2022). *Woman without shame: Poems*. New York: Knopf.

Clark-Louque, A. R., Lindsay, R. B., Quezada, R. L., & Jew, C. L. (2019). *Equity partnerships: A culturally proficient guide to family, school, and community engagement*. Thousand Oaks, CA: Corwin.

Clinton, W. (2021). *Inclusive leadership* [MOOC]. MasterClass. Accessed at www.masterclass.com /classes/president-bill-clinton-teaches-inclusive-leadership on April 26, 2023.

Constantino, S. M. (2016). *Engage every family: Five simple principles*. Thousand Oaks, CA: Corwin.

Constantino, S. M. (2021). *Engage every family: Five simple principles* (2nd ed.). Thousand Oaks, CA: Corwin.

Conzemius, A., & O'Neill, J. (2005). *The Power of SMART goals*. Bloomington, IN: Solution Tree Press.

Cooper, C. W. (2009). Parent involvement, African American mothers, and the politics of educational care. *Equity & Excellence in Education*, *42*(4), 379–394.

Covey, S. R. (2008). *The speed of trust: The one thing that changes everything*. New York: Free Press.

Covey, S. R. (2020). *The 7 habits of highly effective people* (30th anniversary ed.). New York: Simon & Schuster.

Creekmore, N., & Creekmore, M. (2022, July 11). How to make your school psychologically safe. *Educational Leadership*, *79*(9). Accessed at www.ascd.org/el/articles/how-to-make-your -school-psychologically-safe on July 19, 2023.

Delgado Gaitan, C. (2004). *Involving Latino families in schools: Raising student achievement through home-school partnerships*. Thousand Oaks, CA: Corwin.

Delpit, L. (1995). *Other people's children: Cultural conflict in the classroom*. New York: The New Press.

DeParle, J. (2023, April 7). Safety net barriers add to child poverty in immigrant families. *The New York Times*. Accessed at www.nytimes.com/2023/04/06/us/politics/child-poverty-immigrants.html on July 28, 2023.

Desmond, M. (2023). *Poverty, by America*. New York: Crown.

Dowd, A. J., Friedlander, E., Jonason, C., Leer, J., Sorensen, L. Z., Guajardo, J., et al. (2017). Lifewide learning for early reading development. *New Directions for Child and Adolescent Development, 2017*(155), 31–49.

DuFour, R., & Eaker, R. (1998). *Professional Learning Communities at Work: Best practices for enhancing student achievement*. Bloomington, IN: Solution Tree Press.

DuFour, R., DuFour, R., Eaker, R., Many, T. W., & Mattos, M. (2016). *Learning by doing: A handbook for Professional Learning Communities at Work* (3rd ed.). Bloomington, IN: Solution Tree Press.

Dugan, J. (2022, September). Co-constructing family engagement. *Educational Leadership, 80*(1), 20–26.

Duhigg, C. (2014). *The power of habit: Why we do what we do in life and business*. New York: Random House.

Duhigg, C. (2016, February 25). What Google learned from its quest to become the perfect team. *New York Times Magazine*. Accessed at www.nytimes.com/2016/02/28/magazine/what-google-learned-from-its-quest-to-build-the-perfect-team.html on July 19, 2023.

Eakins, S. (n.d.). *Families and Educators Together Project with Dr. Kristen Davidson and Ms. Madeleine Case* [Podcast]. Leading Equity. Accessed at www.leadingequitycenter.com/53 on August 22, 2022.

Edmondson, A. C. (2019). *The fearless organization: Creating psychological safety in the workplace for learning, innovation, and growth*. New York: Wiley.

El Yaafouri, L. (2022, September). Doing better by refugee and immigrant families. *Educational Leadership, 80*(1), 43–48.

Epstein, J. L., & Associates. (2018). *School, family, and community partnerships: Your handbook for action* (4th ed.). Thousand Oaks, CA: Corwin.

Facilitate. (n.d.). In *Online etymology dictionary*. Accessed at www.etymonline.com/word/facilitate on August 15, 2023.

Ferlazzo, L. (2011, May). Involvement or engagement? Schools, families, communities. *Educational Leadership, 68*(8), 10–14.

Fisher, D., & Frey, N. (2022, September). Community circles build restorative school cultures. *Educational Leadership, 80*(1), 74–75.

Fosslien, L. (2022). *Diversity is having a seat at the table, inclusion is having a voice, and belonging is having that voice be* [Post]. LinkedIn. Accessed at www.linkedin.com/posts/liz-fosslien_diversity-is-having-a-seat-at-the-table-activity-6917946008253472768-IJxk?utm_source=linkedin_share&utm_medium=member_desktop_web on December 19, 2022.

Freire, P. (2018). *Pedagogy of the oppressed* (50th anniversary ed.; M. B. Ramos, Trans.). London: Bloomsbury Academic.

Fullan, M. (2007). *The new meaning of educational change* (4th ed.). New York: Teachers College Press.

Fullan, M. (2011). *The six secrets of change: What the best leaders do to help their organizations survive and thrive.* San Francisco: Jossey-Bass.

Garcia, M. E., Frunzi, K., Dean, C. B., Flores, N., & Miller, K. B. (2016, September). *Toolkit of resources for engaging families and the community as partners in education part 1: Building an understanding of family and community engagement.* Washington, DC: U.S. Department of Education. Accessed at https://files.eric.ed.gov/fulltext/ED569110.pdf on August 21, 2022.

Garcia, N. (2017, October 4). *Denver, Boulder schools home to the state's largest achievement gaps based on race, new data shows.* Accessed at https://co.chalkbeat.org/2017/10/4/21103505/denver -boulder-schools-home-to-the-state-s-largest-achievement-gaps-based-on-race-new-data -shows on July 6, 2023.

Gawlik, K., & Melynk, B. M. (2022, May). *Pandemic parenting: Examining the epidemic of working parental burnout and strategies to help.* Accessed at https://wellness.osu.edu/sites /default/files/documents/2022/05/OCWO_ParentalBurnout_3674200_Report_FINAL.pdf on April 24, 2023.

Gibbs, J. (2006). *Tribes learning communities.* Windsor, CA: CenterSource Systems.

Goodwin, B., & Gibson, T. (2022, September). Making families happy: Three ways school leaders can foster family relations. *Educational Leadership, 80*(1), 82–83.

Hamilton, D. M. (2013). *Everything is workable: A Zen approach to conflict resolution.* Boulder, CO: Shambhala.

Hamilton, D. M., Wilson, G. M., & Loh, K. (2020). *Compassionate conversations: How to speak and listen from the heart.* Boulder, CO: Shambhala.

Hanushek, E. (2022, August 26). Finding the best teachers for post-pandemic schools. *The Wall Street Journal.* Accessed at www.wsj.com/articles/finding-the-best-teachers-for-post-pandemic -schools-11661522193 on July 27, 2023.

Heath, C., & Heath, D. (2010). *Switch: How to change things when change is hard.* New York: Crown Business.

Henderson A. T., & Mapp, K. L. (2002). *A new wave of evidence: The impact of school, family, and community connections on student achievement.* Austin, TX: National Center for Family & Community Connections With Schools.

Henderson, A. T., Mapp, K. L., Johnson, V. R., & Davies, D. (2007). *Beyond the bake sale: The essential guide to family/school partnerships.* New York: The New Press.

Hong, S. (2019). *Natural allies: Hope and possibility in teacher-family partnerships.* Cambridge, MA: Harvard Education Press.

Ishimaru, A. M. (2018). Re-imagining turnaround: Families and communities leading educational justice. *Journal of Educational Administration, 56*(5), 546–561.

Ishimaru, A. M. (2020). *Just schools: Building equitable collaborations with families and communities.* New York: Teachers College Press.

Ishimaru, A. M., Bang, M., & Valladares, M. (2019, December 11). *5 new ways for schools to work with families*. Accessed at https://theconversation.com/5-new-ways-for-schools-to-work -with-families-120964 on August 21, 2022.

Jargon, J. (2022, August 13). Why do schools send so many emails? They don't have to. *The Wall Street Journal*. Accessed at www.wsj.com/articles/why-do-schools-send-so-many-emails-they-dont -have-to-11660354530 on July 28, 2023.

Kagan, S., & Kagan, M. (2009). *Kagan cooperative learning*. San Clemente, CA: Authors.

Kamenetz, A. (2022). *The stolen year: How COVID changed children's lives, and where we go now*. New York: PublicAffairs.

Kane, T., & Reardon, S. (2023, May 11). Parents don't understand how far behind their kids are. *The New York Times*. Accessed at www.nytimes.com/interactive/2023/05/11/opinion/pandemic -learning-losses-steep-but-not-permanent.html on July 26, 2023.

Kegan, R., & Lahey, L. L. (2016). *An everyone culture: Becoming a deliberately developmental organization*. Boston: Harvard Business Review Press.

Keller, G. (2013). *The ONE thing: The surprisingly simple truth behind extraordinary results*. Hudson Bend, TX: Bard Press.

Kessler, R. (2000). *The soul of education: Helping students find connection, compassion, and character at school*. Alexandria, VA: ASCD.

Kiddle, R. (2021). *Whakawhanaungatanga* as a blueprint for radical social transformation. In P. Clayton, K. M. Archie, J. Sachs, & E. Steiner (Eds.), *The new possible: Visions of our world beyond crisis* (pp. 240–246). Eugene, OR: Cascade Books.

Kim, Y. (2009). Minority parental involvement and school barriers: Moving the focus away from deficiencies of parents. *Educational Research Review, 4*(2), 80–102.

Kise, J. A. G., & Holm, A. C. (2022). *Educator bandwidth: How to reclaim your energy, passion, and time*. Alexandria, VA: ASCD.

Klein, A. (2021, September 14). Pandemic parents are more engaged. How can schools keep it going? *Education Week*. Accessed at www.edweek.org/leadership/pandemic-parents-are-more -engaged-how-can-schools-keep-it-going/2021/09 on July 19, 2023.

Knight, J. (2022). *The definitive guide to instructional coaching: Seven factors for success*. Alexandria, VA: ASCD.

Koralek, D., Nemeth, K., & Ramsey, K. (2019). *Families and educators together: Building great relationships that support young children*. Washington, DC: National Association for the Education of Young Children.

Kraft, M. A., & Dougherty, S. M. (2013). The effect of teacher-family communication on student engagement: Evidence from a randomized field experiment. *Journal of Research on Educational Effectiveness, 6*(3), 199–222.

Krownapple, J. (2017). *Guiding teams to excellence with equity: Culturally proficient facilitation*. Thousand Oaks, CA: Corwin.

Kurtz, H. (2022, April 14). A profession in crisis: Findings from a national teacher survey. *Education Week*. Accessed at www.edweek.org/research-center/reports/teaching-profession-in-crisis-national-teacher-survey on August 21, 2022.

Lantieri, L. (Ed.). (2001). *Schools with spirit: Nurturing the inner lives of students and teachers*. Boston: Beacon Press.

Laskowski, T. (2023, March 1). In organizational change efforts, belonging matters. *Educational Leadership, 80*(6). Accessed at www.ascd.org/el/articles/in-organizational-change-efforts-belonging-matters on August 23, 2023.

Lawrence-Lightfoot, S. (2004). *The essential conversation: What parents and teachers can learn from each other*. New York: Ballantine.

Learning Heroes. (2021, December 8). *Parents 2021: Going beyond the headlines. Responding to what parents, teachers, & principals really want* [Slide presentation]. Accessed at https://bealearninghero.org/wp-content/uploads/2021/12/Parents-2021.pdf on August 17, 2022.

Lesser, M. (2019). *Seven practices of a mindful leader: Lessons from Google and a Zen monastery kitchen*. Novato, CA: New World Library.

Loehr, J., & Schwartz, T. (2005). *The power of full engagement: Managing energy, not time, is the key to high performance and personal renewal*. New York: Free Press.

Love, B. L. (2021, January 12). How to make anti-racism more than a performance. *Education Week*. Accessed at www.edweek.org/leadership/opinion-empty-promises-of-equity/2021/01 on August 21, 2022.

Mahler, J. (2023, April 28). The most dangerous person in the world is Randi Weingarten. *New York Times Magazine*. Accessed at www.nytimes.com/2023/04/28/magazine/randi-weingarten-teachers-unions.html on July 28, 2023.

Mapp, K. L. (2021, March 25). *Race, equity and the future of school* [Online symposium]. Equal Opportunity Schools, Seattle, WA.

Mapp, K. L., & Bergman, E. (2021). *Embracing a new normal: Toward a more liberatory approach to family engagement*. Accessed at www.carnegie.org/publications/embracing-new-normal-toward-more-liberatory-approach-family-engagement/ on August 21, 2023.

Mapp, K. L., Carver, I., & Lander, J. (2017). *Powerful partnerships: A teacher's guide to engaging families for student success*. New York: Scholastic.

Mapp, K. L., Henderson, A., Cuevas, S., Franco, M., & Ewert, S. (2022). *Everyone wins! The evidence for family-school partnerships and implications for practice*. New York: Scholastic.

Marschall, M. J. (2006). Parent involvement and educational outcomes for Latino students. *Review of Policy Research, 23*(5), 1053–1076.

Marzano, R. J. (2000). *A new era of school reform: Going where the research takes us*. Aurora, CO: Mid-Continent Research for Education and Learning.

McKeown, G. (2014). *Essentialism: The disciplined pursuit of less*. New York: Crown Business.

Meckler, L., & Rabinowitz, K. (2019, December 27). America's schools are more diverse than ever. But the teachers are still mostly white. *The Washington Post.* Accessed at www.washingtonpost .com/graphics/2019/local/education/teacher-diversity on July 19, 2023.

MetLife. (2013, February 21). *The MetLife survey of the American teacher: Challenges for school leadership.* Accessed at www.metlife.com/about-us/newsroom/2013/february/the-metlife-survey -of-the-american-teacher--challenges-for-schoo/ on August 21, 2022.

Michail, J. (2020, August 24). Strong nonverbal skills matter now more than ever in this "new normal." *Forbes.* Accessed at www.forbes.com/sites/forbescoachescouncil/2020/08/24/strong-nonverbal -skills-matter-now-more-than-ever-in-this-new-normal/?sh=4b6b3db85c61 on October 22, 2022.

Miller, C. C., & Pallaro, B. (2022, June 20). 362 school counselors on pandemic's harm. *The New York Times,* p. A15.

Miller-Muro, L. (2023). Deliberate: Body language [Course lecture]. In *Meeting facilitation skills for leaders of diverse teams* [MOOC]. Accessed at www.udemy.com/course/inclusive-facilitation -skills-for-leaders-of-diverse-teams/ on July 17, 2023.

Natanson, H., Stein, P., & Asbury, N. (2022, July 15). D.C.-area schools see spike in teacher resignations. *The Washington Post.* Accessed at www.washingtonpost.com/education/2022/07/15 /teacher-resignations-rise-dc-area on July 19, 2023.

National Association for Family, School, and Community Engagement. (2020a, September). *State of the states: Family, school, and community engagement within state educator licensure requirements.* Accessed at https://nafsce.org/page/stateofthestates on November 27, 2022.

National Association for Family, School, and Community Engagement. (2020b, July). *Survey: Family engagement during COVID-19.* Accessed at https://nafsce.org/page/covid19survey on November 27, 2022.

National Center for Education Statistics. (2022). *Explore achievement gaps data.* Accessed at https://nces.ed.gov/nationsreportcard/studies/gaps on July 6, 2023.

Noguera, P. (2018, July 25). *The role of leadership in promoting equity and countering racial inequality in education* [Public comments]. Colorado Association of School Executives (CASE) Convention, Beaver Creek.

Noguera, P. (2021, March 26). *Creating equity in schools.* Equity Virtual Summit. Accessed at https://m.facebook.com/accutraink12/videos/dr-pedro-noguera-3-steps-to-equity-in-schools -virtual-summit-326/313121926815887/?__so__=permalink&__rv__=related_videos& locale=zh_CN.] on July 20, 2023.

Nomensen, T. (2018). *Teacher talk: How many White, middle-class, female educators perpetuate White privilege in school* (Publication No. 770) [Doctoral dissertation, University of Missouri-St. Louis]. IRL@ University of Missouri-St. Louis. Accessed at https://irl.umsl.edu/dissertation/770 on July 17, 2023.

O'Donohue, J. (2018). *Walking in wonder: Eternal wisdom for a modern world.* New York: Convergent.

Oliveira, G. (2022, September 4). What is school for? For hope. *The New York Times,* p. SR9.

Palmer, P. J. (1998). *The courage to teach: Exploring the inner landscape of a teacher's life.* San Francisco: Jossey-Bass.

Palmer, P. J. (2004). *A hidden wholeness: The journey toward an undivided life.* San Francisco: Jossey-Bass.

Parker, P. (2018). *The art of gathering: How we meet and why it matters.* New York: Riverhead Books.

Passageworks Institute. (2015). *Foundations course trainer's manual* [Unpublished manuscript]. Boulder, CO: Passageworks Institute.

Payne, C. M. (2008). *So much reform, so little change: The persistence of failure in urban schools.* Cambridge, MA: Harvard Education Press.

Pfeffer, J., & Sutton, R. I. (2006). *Hard facts, dangerous half-truths, and total nonsense: Profiting from evidence-based management.* Cambridge, MA: Harvard Business School Press.

Pondiscio, R. (2022, September). Schools must rebuild trust. *Educational Leadership, 80*(1), 64–67.

Posey-Maddox, L., & Haley-Lock, A. (2020). One size does not fit all: Understanding parent engagement in the contexts of work, family, and public schooling. *Urban Education, 55*(5), 671–698. https://doi.org/10.1177/0042085916660348

PTA Family-School Partnerships. (2019). *PTA national standards for family-school partnerships: An implementation guide.* Accessed at www.pta.org/docs/default-source/files/runyourpta/national-standards/national_standards_implementation_guide.pdf on September 13, 2022.

Rebora, A. (2022, September). Family engagement reimagined. *Educational Leadership, 80*(1), 7.

Robbins, A. (2023). *The teachers: A year inside America's most vulnerable, important profession.* New York: Dutton.

Robbins, T. (1991). *Awaken the giant within: How to take immediate control of your mental, emotional, physical and financial destiny!* New York: Simon & Schuster.

Robinson, K. (2009). *The element: How finding your passion changes everything.* New York: Penguin.

Sanders, M. G., & Sheldon, S. B. (2016). *Principals matter: A guide to school, family, and community partnerships.* New York: Skyhorse.

Santana, L., Rothstein, D., & Bain, A. (2016). *Partnering with parents to ask the right questions: A powerful strategy for strengthening school-family partnerships.* Alexandria, VA: ASCD.

Santelises, S. B. (2020, December 1). Parents are watching like never before. "Trust us" isn't enough. *Education Week.* Accessed at www.edweek.org/teaching-learning/opinion-parents-are-watching-like-never-before-trust-us-isnt-enough/2020/12 on April 25, 2023.

Schaedel, B., Freund, A., Azaiza, F., Hertz-Lazarowitz, R., Boem, A., & Eshet, Y. (2015). School climate and teachers' perceptions of parental involvement in Jewish and Arab primary schools in Israel. *International Journal About Parents in Education, 9*(1), 77–92.

Schultz, K. (2019). *Distrust and educational change: Overcoming barriers to just and lasting reform.* Cambridge, MA: Harvard Education Press.

Senge, P. M. (1990). *The fifth discipline: The art and practice of the learning organization.* New York: Doubleday.

Senge, P. M. (2000). *Schools that learn: A fifth discipline fieldbook for educators, parents and everyone who cares about education.* New York: Knopf.

Sheldon, S. (2021, April 16). *Family, school, community partnerships evaluation* [Presentation]. Colorado Department of Education, Denver.

Shirley, D. (1997). *Community organizing for urban school reform.* Austin: University of Texas Press.

Sinek, S. (2011). *Start with why: How great leaders inspire everyone to take action.* New York: Portfolio.

Singal, J. (2023, January 17). What if diversity trainings do more harm than good? *The New York Times.* Accessed at www.nytimes.com/2023/01/17/opinion/dei-trainings-effective.html on January 28, 2023.

Singh, K. D. (2022, August 17). Clean toilets and inspired teachers and students: How India's capital is fixing its public schools. *The New York Times.* Accessed at www.nytimes.com/2022/08/16/world/asia/india-delhi-schools.html on July 26, 2023.

Stanton-Salazar, R. D. (2011). A social capital framework for the study of institutional agents and their role in the empowerment of low-status students and youth. *Youth & Society, 43*(3), 1066–1109.

St. George, D. (2022, July 6). Behavioral issues, absenteeism at schools increase, federal data shows. *The Washington Post.* Accessed at www.washingtonpost.com/education/2022/07/05/absenteeism-behavioral-issues-pandemic-data on July 19, 2023.

Stone, G. W. (2017, October 18). These are the happiest cities in the United States. *National Geographic.* Accessed at www.nationalgeographic.com/travel/article/happiest-cities-united-states-2017 on August 20, 2022.

Suskind, D. (2022). *Parent nation: Unlocking every child's potential, fulfilling society's promise.* New York: Dutton.

Tschannen-Moran, M. (2014). *Trust matters: Leadership for successful schools* (2nd ed.). San Francisco: Jossey-Bass.

Turney, K., & Kao, G. (2009). Barriers to school involvement: Are immigrant parents disadvantaged? *The Journal of Educational Research, 102*(4), 257–271.

Understood & UnidosUS. (2021, July 30). *2021 back to school study* [Slide presentation]. Accessed at https://assets.ctfassets.net/p0qf7j048i0q/27Ojdfhmo5hhLHfeiyVA0E/55e6fd2231eeeb9ee1456676eb3de947/Back_to_School_Study.pdf on July 20, 2023.

UnidosUS. (2022). *Latino student success: Advancing U.S. educational progress for all.* Accessed at www.unidosus.org/wp-content/uploads/2022/07/UnidosUS_Latino-Education_2022.pdf on April 25, 2023.

Valdés, G. (1996). *Con respeto: Bridging the distances between culturally diverse families and schools: An ethnographic portrait.* New York: Teachers College Press.

Valenzuela, A. (2017). *Subtractive schooling: U.S.-Mexican youth and the politics of caring.* Albany: State University of New York Press.

Walker, T. (2022, February 1). Survey: Alarming number of educators may soon leave the profession. *NEA Today.* Accessed at www.nea.org/advocating-for-change/new-from-nea/survey-alarming-number-educators-may-soon-leave-profession on August 24, 2022.

Weaver, L., & Wilding, M. (2013). *The 5 dimensions of engaged teaching: A practical guide for educators.* Bloomington, IN: Solution Tree Press.

Weiss, H. B., Lopez, M. E., & Caspe, M. (2018). *Joining together to create a bold vision for next generation family engagement: Engaging families to transform education*. Accessed at www.carnegie .org/publications/joining-together-create-bold-vision-next-generation-family-engagement -engaging-families-transform-education on August 21, 2022.

Weller, F. (2015). *The wild edge of sorrow: Rituals of renewal and the sacred work of grief*. Berkeley, CA: North Atlantic Books.

Wheatley, M. J. (2009). *Turning to one another: Simple conversations to restore hope to the future* (2nd ed.). San Francisco: Berrett-Koehler.

Wilkerson, D., & Kim, H. W. (2010). "We have a lot of sleeping parents": Comparing inner-city and suburban high school teachers' experiences with parent involvement. *Advances in Social Work*, *11*(2), 144–157.

Wilson, S. (2021, October 15). *Reframing family school community partnerships* [Presentation]. Colorado Department of Education, Denver.

Winthrop, R. (2022, January 26). *Top 5 insights for improving family-school collaboration during COVID and beyond* [Blog post]. Accessed at www.brookings.edu/blog/education -plus-development/2022/01/26/top-5-insights-for-improving-family-school-collaboration -during-covid-and-beyond on December 11, 2022.

Winthrop, R., Barton, A., Ershadi, M., & Ziegler, L. (2021). *Collaborating to transform and improve education systems: A playbook for family-school engagement*. Accessed at www.brookings .edu/essay/collaborating-to-transform-and-improve-education-systems-a-playbook-for-family -school-engagement on August 18, 2022.

Woolley, K., & Fishbach, A. (2017). A recipe for friendship: Similar food consumption promotes trust and cooperation. *Journal of Consumer Psychology*, *27*(1), 1–10. https://doi.org/10.1016/j.jcps. 2016.06.003

Zeichner, K., Bowman, M., Guillen, L., & Napolitan, K. (2016, July 20). Engaging and working in solidarity with local communities in preparing the teachers of their children. *Journal of Teacher Education*, *67*(4). https://doi.org/10.1177/0022487116660623

INDEX

Parentships in a PLC at Work®
Kyle Palmer
Kyle Palmer draws from his experience both as a principal of a model PLC school and as a parent to offer practical strategies for including parents or guardians as part of your collaborative culture focused on student learning.
BKG021

The Wraparound Guide
Leigh Colburn and Linda Beggs
Your school has the power to help students overcome barriers to well-being and achievement—from mental health issues to substance abuse to trauma. With this timely guide, discover actionable steps for launching and sustaining wraparound services embedded within your school that support the whole child.
BKF956

Leading the Launch
Kim Wallace
How do schools and districts make true progress? One step at a time. *Leading the Launch* offers a ten-stage initiative implementation process proven to help you lead the charge for change with ingenuity, flexibility, responsiveness, and passion.
BKG030

Beyond Conversations About Race
Washington Collado, Sharroky Hollie, Rosa Isiah, Yvette Jackson, Anthony Muhammad, Douglas Reeves, and Kenneth C. Williams
Written by a collective of brilliant authors, this essential work provokes respectful dialogue about race that catalyzes school-changing action. The book masterfully weaves together an array of scenarios, discussions, and challenging topics to help prepare all of us to do better in our schools and communities.
BKG035

Solution Tree | Press
a division of
Solution Tree

Visit SolutionTree.com or call 800.733.6786 to order.